This is Our Faith

This is Our Faith

Bishop
Maurice Wood

HODDER AND STOUGHTON
LONDON SYDNEY AUCKLAND TORONTO

British Library Cataloguing in Publication Data
Wood, Maurice A. P.
 This is our faith.
 1. Theology, Doctrinal
 I. Title
 230   BT77.3

 ISBN 0 340 38602 9

*Hodder and Stoughton Editorial Office: 47 Bedford Square, London
WC1B 3DP.*

Dedicated to the
clergy and people of the
ancient and lively Diocese
of
NORWICH
which Margaret, my wife,
and I have been
privileged to love and
serve for 14 years

CONTENTS

This is the faith of the Church.
This is our faith.
We believe and trust in one God,
Father, Son, and Holy Spirit.

ASB Confirmation Service

FOREWORD

I believe a bishop is ordained at his consecration to be a guardian of the Faith and of the flock of Christ. So this book is offered to all Christians, perhaps struggling with doubt, crippled by a sense of insufficiency, but wanting to be sure of Christ, so they may serve him better.

This book is also offered to sincere seekers, who want to find a sure grasp of the historic Christian Faith, and to be freed from unnecessary doubts into self-forgetful service in their own day and generation. I am writing this book as a bishop, desiring to be an enabler, in the spirit of Paul who wrote to Timothy: "My son, be strong in the grace that is in Christ Jesus, and what you have heard from me, before many witnesses, entrust to faithful men, who will be able to teach others also" (2 Tim. 2:1, 2 RSV).

Because bishops are "not to be novices, or recent converts" (1 Tim. 3:6) with a care for the family of the Church, likened to the faith of a household "for if a man does not know how to manage his own household, how can he care for God's church?" (1 Tim. 3:5), this means that bishops are usually fairly senior in years, except for the lively example of our young Anglican bishops in missionary situations in South America. Their task is not to do all the work themselves, but to ensure they are handing on the fulness and glory of the Christian Faith to younger generations in their shepherdly care. Perhaps for this reason I have particularly enjoyed visiting schools, both church and county ones, confirming at boarding schools and at our University of East Anglia and commissioning

9

hundreds of Sunday School teachers and licensing lay readers, in the knowledge that I am following in the steps of St. Felix (AD 630) and St. Furzey (from Ireland in AD 673) and the long line of East Anglian shepherd-bishops who have not only held the Faith of Christ, but striven to hand it on in all its fulness and freshness to generations to come.

With particular affection, then, I pray this book may sum up the teaching ministry that I and my fellow bishops are constantly engaged in as I offer it, also, to all in the diocese of Norwich, whom I have sought to serve, so that in the words of our "Call to Mission Prayer" made in 1973 "we may know Christ better, and make him better known, by yielding our wills to the service of Christ, and our lives to the service of others."

MAURICE NORVIC

The Bishop's House, Norwich

St Barnabas' Day, June 11th 1985

1

FAITH UNDER FIRE

The Christian Faith seems seriously threatened today, especially the Faith as it is held in the Church of England, revealed in the Bible, and proclaimed in its Creeds, which are the Creeds of the Universal Church. Every bishop and priest at his ordination is called to a solemn and sincere assent of the Christian Faith. This is summarised in the "Declaration of Assent", which is also used again, before any bishop or clergyman swears allegiance to the Crown and obedience to his archbishop or bishop. He also states before the Christian people he is called to serve, that in Christ's Name, he will uphold this Faith.

How serious then is the threat to the Christian Faith today, "as the Church of England has received it"?

There has been a rumbling anxiety in the Church since a television programme early in 1984, called *Credo* (which means "I believe"), which brought some apparently "off the cuff" reactions, querying the received truths about Christ's Resurrection, from the Reverend Dr. David Jenkins, Professor of Theology at Leeds University. He had just been nominated, on the advice of the Crown Appointments Commission of the General Synod, to succeed the Archbishop of York as Bishop of Durham.

Dr. Jenkins said, "I hold the view that he, Jesus, rose from the dead. The question is what that means, isn't it? Now I think I would like to say that it doesn't seem to me, reading the records as they remain in the Gospels, and what Paul says in 1 Corinthians, that *there was any one event* which you could identify with 'the Resurrection'.

11

What seems to me to have happened, is that there was a series of experiences, which convinced – gradually convinced – a growing number of the people who became apostles, that Jesus had certainly been dead, certainly buried and he wasn't finished. What is more, he wasn't just not finished, but he was raised up. That is to say, the very life and power and purpose and personality which was in him, was actually continuing and was continuing both in the sphere of God and in the sphere of history, so that he was a risen and living presence and personality."

It sounded like a mild modernism, reflecting the negative critical scholarship of the 1920s, but for two factors. First, it became apparent that Dr. Jenkins had *not* stated his belief (a) that Jesus was physically raised from the dead (b) that the decisive resurrection event took place "on the third day" and (c) that Mary, Peter and the Twelve actually saw him in his risen body, alike in continuity, but transformed in his new resurrection body, and that this was their immediate testimony, although "some doubted" (Matt. 28:17).

The more it became apparent that what he had *not* said, and what he appeared unwilling to say, was his true position, the more anxiety about his consecration as a bishop who is a guardian of the Faith, increased, with widespread and public concern.

If this had been said by one of the well-known speculative and radical theologians like Don Cupitt who, with Dennis Nineham, Maurice Wiles and John Hick, the Professor of Theology at Birmingham University, contributed to the provocatively titled book *The Myth of God Incarnate* (SCM Press, 1972), Dr. Jenkins' words might have passed unremarked. But Dr. David Jenkins suddenly found himself being reported, not as an academic, but as a bishop-designate, and one who would become at once the senior diocesan bishop in the Northern Province of York, without the benefit of learning the bishop's job first, as a suffragan, or as the bishop of a smaller diocese.

At first, most of us, his brother bishops, sought to "close ranks" and gave him the benefit of the doubt, and we remembered, sometimes with wry painfulness, the first things we ourselves had said in the early heady days of our own public lives as diocesan bishops. "Remember," said a wise senior bishop to me, fourteen years before, at my own consecration, "a bishop always has a microphone clipped to his cassock."

Secondly, it slowly became clear that these apparently "off the cuff" assertions, and reservations, reflected Dr. Jenkins' settled views, and he appeared unable or unwilling to profess more clearly the crucial statements of the Faith of the Church.

Thirdly, the possibility that perhaps some other bishops could be persuaded to make equivocal statements led to a spate of T.V. programmes, interviews, and news items, throughout 1984, highlighted by petitions that Dr. Jenkins, unless he could openly and whole-heartedly affirm the historic statements of the Creed, should *not* be consecrated in York Minster, before the General Synod which happened to be meeting in York was convened. Questions were then asked in Synod; and by the Archbishop of York's relevant and contemporary sermon on "murmurings" on Sunday. Then, before dawn on the very next day, as the archbishop was about to fly out to the World Council of Churches meeting in Geneva, where for a number of years Dr. Jenkins had been on the staff, York Minster was struck by lightning and caught fire.

I give this condensed reference to the dramatic events of the summer of 1984, as briefly and factually as possible, not to over-dramatise, but to underline the fact that the rumbling question marks about doubt and faith, publicly sparked off by Dr. David Jenkins' earlier remarks, have continued to be heard for well over a year. To my certain knowledge, from letters, interviews, press and radio and T.V. requests for comments, I know sadly that straight-forward rank and file members of the Church of England, and members of other churches, have been troubled by what appears to be the uncertain voice of some in positions of episcopal leadership, and guardianship of the historic Christian Faith.

Although, later in this book, I make specific reference to some of the things which the present Bishop of Durham has written, more fully, after the early *Credo* programme, and I state my reasons for assenting to the traditional Church of England doctrines, this book is not designed to be confrontational.

I write for the future, because I believe that the motto *"Veritas vincit"* which states that Truth always conquers is true. I believe, from my own personal experience, that when Jesus said "I am the Truth", he was revealing in his own divine Person, but within the context of our common humanity, which he shared with us "yet without sin", all the basic and gathered truths that God, his Heavenly Father, wants us to know. In his death and Resurrection, he draws us to himself, and in the forgiveness of our sins, he removes the veils of doubt and pride and rebellion from our eyes. In his God-ordained Resurrection, he opens the door for our entry into newness of life, by his Holy Spirit. By that same Spirit, who inbreathed the varied personalities of the human authors, whose work the Church then recognised as the Canonical Scriptures of Old and New Testament, we discover with humble assurance "the Truth as it is in Jesus" (Eph. 4:21). When we read the Bible daily, our faith grows, our knowledge deepens and our experience of meeting Jesus the Living Word of God in the Bible, matures. Thus we not only grow in grace and in the fellowship of his Church, but we are equipped for resolute and unselfish service in the world. We are called to fulfil Christ's final command, given after his glorious Resurrection, to "Go into all the world, and make disciples of all nations, baptising them into the name of God, Father, Son and Holy Spirit" (Matt. 28:19).

Therefore, at the climax of fourteen years as a diocesan bishop, soon to move to the wider work of a retired bishop in the Church, I write for the future, to help, encourage and strengthen all those young and old, whom I have been privileged to serve as a guardian of the Faith.

I believe we must ask: How serious is this threat to the

Faith, posed by the present negative emphases on doubting the historic affirmation of the Catholic Faith, as it is revealed in Scripture, and as it has sustained generations of ordinary Christians, down the centuries? With that great Anglican divine Richard Hooker we need to take a central view. We should not underestimate the threat, nor should we overstate it, because "our God reigns".

Is this just a domestic issue in the Church of England?

The alleged doubts about Christ's bodily Resurrection are a matter of discussion and concern well beyond the Church of England, and the Archbishop of Canterbury said to us in the House of Bishops in a statement later made public to the Press, that because he had received a very large number of letters, questioning the alleged orthodoxy of us bishops, on a "guilt by association, if not disavowed" theory, he had stated openly that "the doctrines of the Incarnation and the Resurrection are not in doubt amongst the bishops . . . The Church of God has a gospel to proclaim and a faith to affirm . . . To be a Christian is to worship and obey Jesus as Lord . . ." Nonetheless persistent questions were asked in the General Synod in July 1984 and again in November 1984, and this led to the major debate on doctrine in the General Synod in February 1985 on the limits of the traditional comprehensiveness of the Church of England. The seriousness of the doubts about our episcopal orthodoxy as guardians of the Faith was voiced by one Synodsman from the North (Revd. David Holloway) who said: "We are living in a crisis time for the Church of England and we have a crisis of confidence in the leadership of the Church. What is now needed is a clear statement from the bishops. Thinking people are not impressed at being told that the doctrines of the Incarnation and the Resurrection are not in doubt among the bishops, when they know that the bishops are re-defining these doctrines so as to exclude the Virgin Birth and the empty tomb." Drawing attention to earlier controversies, Mr. Holloway reminded the General Synod of Archbishop William Temple who in 1938 said, "In view of my own responsibility in the Church, I think it right here to affirm that I whole-heartedly accept as historical facts the birth of our Lord from a virgin mother and the Resurrection of his physical body from death and the tomb." As Bishop Westcott, a former Bishop of Durham and a great New Testament scholar, put it when referring to the bodily Resurrection of Jesus, "The Resurrection is either a miracle or an illusion. If the Resurrection be unhistoric, they (the apostles) were deceived . . . The Resurrection of Jesus Christ is not some formula to be played around with or re-defined by the House of Bishops. It is the heart of the Gospel."

Because the Church of England is the National Church, this issue of doubt and faith is not confined to our domestic discussions, and because a bishop airing doubts is news, and bishops upholding orthodoxy in their various diocesan magazines is *not* news, the distress caused went far beyond the domestic life of the professional clergy. Because the media are interested in news, rather than freely disseminating the Faith, unease became widespread amongst very many regular church-goers, and fringe members, for whom as the Church of the Nation we have, I believe, a real responsibility for gentle pastoral care.

Is this just a "party" issue in the Church?

Before I made a public statement on this issue in Holy Week of 1985, I searched my mind and conscience. My own upbringing in the Christian Faith from my boyhood was enlightened, and broadened and deepened by a personal faith in Jesus Christ, revealed through an assured and regular study of the Bible. This challenged me to the uncomfortable and energetic task of evangelism, amongst boys and girls, students, members of the Royal Navy, Royal Marines and in fifteen years of parish ministry in Oxford and Islington. The assurance of the experience of seeing people, year by year, coming alive to God, through faith in Jesus Christ, has so deepened my belief in the great historic facts of the Faith, that I was not sure that I could enter with full sympathy into the apparent airing of doubts and questions which seemed to mark the methodology of radical and critical teachers.

Did the very convictions of my evangelical and biblical inheritance, and this day-by-day work of parish and personal evangelism, inhibit me from dispassionately assessing those who seemed to teach others by airing their own doubts? This made me slow to speak publicly on this issue.

Ten years in theological education as Principal of Oak Hill Theological College, and finally as Chairman of the Principals' Conference, before I became bishop in 1971, helped me to see that these issues of doubt and faith, which are not new, are not "party" issues at all, but need resolving *before* men are ordained, in the intellectual rigour of the class-room, for there is certainly nothing meritorious in doubt concerning the Christian foundations of our faith, nor are they "party" issues between the evangelical, catholic and liberal streams of church life. I have seen this even more clearly in our Norwich diocese, which has an interesting breadth of tradition. We have the largest number of Scripture Union children's missions around our coasts every summer and Christian youth cruises on the Norfolk Broads. Our bishop's chaplains for holidaymakers, though not all of evangelical persuasion, are united in their evangelistic convictions of sharing the fulness of the Christian Faith with others.

We also have the pilgrimage shrine at Walsingham in our diocese. This was re-established by a senior kinsman of mine, the Reverend Hope Patten, in 1925. It has now become a holy place for prayer and pilgrimage, in the "High Church" tradition. Yet I find that today, our Anglo-Catholic clergy and laity and our evangelical clergy and laity and very many in the Central Church tradition also, are finding a new unity, in a positive affirmation of the Catholic Faith, revealed in the Scriptures, and expounded by the Church, and a resolute and robust rejection of speculative religious doubt. It has been very heartening to see how Christians of all traditions, Anglican, Free Church, and Roman Catholic, were deeply involved in every aspect of our Mission England work in Norfolk. It would be serious if the acids of academic and theoretical doubts about the central tenets of the Faith sapped this growth in grace, and harmed so many young Christians, in the early enthusiasm of their Christian pilgrimage in life.

Certainly this is not simply a "party" matter. A rather charming, though now sorrowful coincidence underlines this. Monkton Combe School, near Bath, was founded over 100 years ago for the sons of clergy, overseas missionaries and officers' families. It has always maintained a robust Christian ethos. A few years ago, and until the sudden death of Bishop David Brown, Monkton Combe School was the only school which had three diocesan bishops together on the Bishops' Benches in the House of Lords: Graham Leonard, of London; David Brown, deeply involved in ecumenical and missionary work, of Guildford; and myself of Norwich. We might be considered "High", "Central" and "Low", but the motto of Monkton Combe School *"Verbum tuum Veritas"*, "Thy Word is Truth", informed all our three ministries. I have much enjoyed reading the Bishop of London's recent book *Firmly I Believe and Truly*, in which from a different perspective, and with a much greater ability than I possess, the bishop, who is the Senior Bishop of the Anglican Communion, re-asserts the great traditional doctrines of the Christian Faith. In doing so he links, as I believe rightly, the need to understand with our minds the great historic facts of the Faith, centring in Christ's unique birth and holy life, his saving death and triumphant Resurrection, with our need of a personal experience of God in Christ. He writes, "Being a Christian is not simply a question of having right beliefs, as if the acceptance by our minds of certain truths by itself was all that matters. To know the only true God and Jesus whom he has sent, is eternal life, not just knowing certain truths. To use a New Testament phrase it is as we 'do the truth' that we come to know God" (page 9, *Firmly I Believe and Truly*, Bishop of London: Mowbray). Yes, indeed, *"Verbum tuum Veritas"*!

Is this simply creative tension in a comprehensive Church?

As a student of modern church history, I realise that tensions between church denominations and also within denominations are part of church life today, and the "doubt/faith syndrome" today has its mirror image in the "traditional/radical syndrome" which, for instance, the Roman Catholic Church in Holland has at the present time, in which the Pope has been appointing conservative bishops to take over liberal dioceses.

Our present tensions have historical roots, also. In the 1960s *Honest to God* might not have been noticed, if it had been written when John Robinson was still teaching theology at Clare College, Cambridge. But even though he was quite a new suffragan bishop, his painful but honest sharing of areas of doubt, and his attempt to express the Faith in contemporary terms however modestly caused a greater stir than he expected, he once told me. But as he was a bishop, people were alerted and listened. In fact Bishop John Robinson was a comparatively traditional theologian in Biblical matters, as shown by his later book on the very early datings for the writing of the three Synoptic Gospels, when he even also placed the writing of the Fourth Gospel before the Sack of Jerusalem (AD 70). A generation before that, much more distress was caused by the rather wild generalisations of Bishop Barnes of Birmingham, which are patently refuted by Sir Frederick Kenyon, in his still important book *The Bible and Modern Scholarship* (John Murray) written in 1948. As the former Director and Principal Librarian of the British Museum, he had easy access to material discovered at Ras Shamra (1929 and onwards). With the Tell El-Amarna letters, and the Chester Beatty papyri, and especially the discovery of the "John Rylands" Fragment of a (small) piece of John's

Gospel, which must be dated between AD 120 and 150, Sir Frederick Kenyon carefully corrects Bishop Barnes' wilder statements. I quote this example, because subconsciously fair-minded readers tend to equate radical statements by speculative academics as scholarly, and traditional statements by pastoral clergymen as "fundamentalist".

The most important historical parallel to our present-day controversies relates to the consecration of Hensley Henson, Dean of Durham, as Bishop of Hereford in 1918, before soon being translated to the See of Durham, in 1920. In Professor Owen Chadwick's scholarly memoir *Hensley Henson: A Study in the Friction between Church and State* (Oxford University Press) an almost similar doctrinal situation arose. Hensley Henson, in his published writings for all to read, has cast doubts on the two great miracles of Christ's coming (the Virgin Birth) and his going (the Bodily Resurrection), but Lloyd George as Prime Minister, and incidentally a Welsh ex-Baptist, was determined to have him as a bishop, because of his undoubted brilliance as a preacher. The Archbishop of Canterbury was so unwilling to consecrate Hensley Henson that he even considered resigning his archbishopric.

Our present circumstances are not dissimilar from those of 1918. Then, there was a Church/State conflict with a prime minister pressing a brilliant man upon an unwilling Archbishop of Canterbury, with strong division amongst the bishops, most of whom either opposed Henson's consecration, or called for an open statement of traditional Christian belief. This put Henson in a very difficult position, if he was still unable to move to a deeper and broader understanding of the essential supernatural truth of our Lord's birth, death and Resurrection.

Years later, another Bishop of Durham, who became another Archbishop of Canterbury, summed it up beautifully and cogently when Archbishop Michael Ramsey wrote, "It is a desperate procedure to try and build a Christian gospel upon the words of Jesus of Galilee, apart from the climax of Calvary, Easter and Pentecost . . . Life-through-death is the principle of Jesus's whole life;

so utterly new and foreign to the expectations of man was this doctrine, that only *historical* events could have created it."

In the end, after much soul-searching on behalf of Archbishop Davidson and Hensley Henson, a careful compromise was reached, in which Henson professed his faith in the Creed and declared he had no wish to alter its words on the Virgin Birth and the Resurrection of Christ.

Are there limits beyond which a bishop, consecrated as a guardian of the Faith, should not go?

To some the comprehensiveness of the Church of England today is its main weakness, and to others it is its chief glory. The Preface of the 1662 Book of Common Prayer shows this kindly comprehension in its opening sentence, as it looks back to the turbulent years, 100 years before, in the Prayer Book of 1549 and 1552:

> It hath been the wisdom of the Church of England, ever since the first compiling of her public Liturgy, to keep the mean, between the two extremes of too much stiffness in refusing and of too much easiness in admitting any variation from it.

Although this refers to liturgy, the ethos of a comprehensive Church runs through church history, and is as broad as the breadth of Scripture itself, but does not go beyond that gentle comprehensiveness. In the thirty years I have been a member of General Synod and its forerunner, the Church Assembly, the two most sustained and lengthy areas of work were liturgical revision, resulting in the Alternative Service Book of 1980, and the revision of the 1603 Canons or "norms" in 1964 and 1969. In both cases long hours were spent on every major issue, and the revised Canon 5 on the doctrine of the Church of England is therefore a very modern statement on the declared mind of the Church:

The doctrine of the Church of England is grounded in the holy Scriptures, and in such teachings of the ancient Fathers and Councils of the Church as are agreeable to the said Scriptures. In particular such doctrine is to be found in the Thirty-nine Articles of Religion, the Book of Common Prayer, and the Ordinal.

The two greatest miracles of Christ's Incarnation, when he entered our world, and of Christ's Resurrection, when God raised him from the dead "on the third day, according to the Scriptures" (1 Cor. 15:4), are at the very heart of the Church's teaching. Unless the miracle of the Resurrection is true, as the Bible unequivocally states, and as we bishops are whole-heartedly committed to proclaim, we fail our people at the most critical stage of their earthly pilgrimage. "If in this life only, we have hoped in Christ, we are of all men most to be pitied. But in fact Christ has been raised from the dead, the first fruits of those who have fallen asleep. For as by a man has come death, by a man has come also the resurrection of the dead." Then Paul sharpens up his teaching, as he states, succinctly: "For as in Adam all die, so also in Christ, shall all be made alive" (1 Cor. 15:19–22 RSV).

I stand in the episcopal tradition of Bishop Gore of Oxford, who invited Dean Hensley Henson to affirm the faith of our Lord's miraculous Incarnation and visible Resurrection. In the same way I invited the present Bishop of Durham, openly and whole-heartedly to affirm at Easter 1985 the truths expressed in the Creed, where we state our belief in "Our Lord Jesus Christ . . . who for us men and for our salvation, came down from heaven, and was incarnate by the Holy Ghost of the Virgin Mary . . . and the third day He rose again according to the Scriptures".

I chose to speak in a secular setting, but in Holy Week before Easter, when the Norwich Rotary Club invited me to bring them an Easter message. I said:

"What are the facts – the sheer drama of Holy Week,

whether we happen to understand or embrace or reject the doctrines concerning these facts?

The basic facts are:

1. The Passover meal.
2. The 'rigged' trial by both Pilate and the High Priest.
3. The cruel mockery, the soldiers and the crowd.
4. The three crosses on the hill of which the central one is the cross of Jesus.
5. The fact of death openly attested by the Jewish centurion, the Roman Governor and the Jewish Elders.
6. The tomb sealed with a stone and a seal and watched over by a twenty-four hour guard and in which, wrapped in a linen shroud, the dead body of Jesus lay. Pilate had released the body to Joseph, who owned the tomb, and Nicodemus a secret disciple of Jesus, who in the crisis stood openly for Christ.

These are the unattested hard historical facts – the facts that today the media discover and with truth and balance declare as surely happening.

There is total agreement about the facts. We now come to the great division. What happened next the Christian Church in all its parts has maintained from that first Easter Day is a sheer God-activated miracle.

The four Gospel writers and Paul in his immediate and early letter to the Corinthians openly, boldly and confidently proclaim that death was not the end; that the body of Jesus did not remain in the tomb and that God worked the supreme miracle of raising his Son, the Saviour of the world, to life again. This life was not only *resuscitation*. Jesus himself had done this when he raised Lazarus back to human life, but was *Resurrection* in that God raised Jesus from the dead on that third day, which we now call Sunday. His risen body had in it the recognisable marks of the nails to remind us that he truly suffered and bore our sins in his own body on the Cross. But his resurrection body had the marks of victory, a newness of life, and demonstrates what the Bible calls the first fruits of those who rise from the dead, because he gives us the promise of our resurrection bodies in heaven one day.

This central theme of the Christian Gospel is of such major importance that Paul in the early letter to the Corinthians states it as centrally crucial and unavoidable if we are to hold to the Faith in its joyous fulness and recognise within it the power to transform our lives into real Christian lives.

Unashamedly I take my stand with Paul, who in the words of the old Authorised Version of our childhood says in 1 Corinthians 15:1–8:

Moreover, brethren, I declare unto you the gospel which I preached unto you, which also ye have received and wherein ye stand;
By which also ye are saved, if ye keep in memory what I preached unto you, unless ye have believed in vain.
For I delivered unto you first of all that which I also received, how that Christ died for our sins according to the scriptures;
And that he was buried, and that he rose again the third day according to the scriptures;
And that he was seen of Cephas, then of the twelve:
After that, he was seen of above 500 brethren at once; of whom the greater part remain unto this present, but some are fallen asleep.
After that, he was seen of James; then of all the apostles.
And last of all he was seen of me also, as of one born out of due time.

But here, this Holy Week, we face a completely new difficulty in the life of the Church and I would go further to say, in the life of the Nation.

Clifford Longley, the Religious Correspondent of *The Times*, wrote an article on Monday in Holy Week called 'Dilemma over Doubting Bishops', which puts not just the new Bishop of Durham, but the rest of us bishops, in the dock, through guilt by association, unless we openly disavow the Bishop of Durham's doubts. I do not see how

I can bring you a traditional Easter Message without publicly disowning parts of the widely publicised Durham statements but I will try to do it as fairly and positively as possible, because I have now met the new bishop three or four times, and sat on the Bishops' Bench with one other bishop to support him in his maiden speech in the House of Lords last month, and as a person I find him to be a friendly man with an attractive personality.

I believe him to be a kind academic man, and a speculative scholar, but nevertheless I believe he should not be a bishop in the Church of England. As Clifford Longley says, 'A bishop's claim to authority is his role in the Church as a *guardian of the Christian faith*. It is not just an authority claimed by him, but an authority granted to him by the faithful.'

Sadly, I have slowly come to believe Clifford Longley's verdict is the right one, when he says, 'To be seen as having repudiated part of that faith is to lose all his authority.'

Bishop David Jenkins has made two recent statements that call in question the very heart of the Christian Gospel, concerning the Resurrection of Jesus Christ.

Firstly, he suggests that the story that the disciples stole the body from the tomb seems a feasible explanation – but this is the very lie that the enemies of Jesus paid the soldiers to put out on the first Easter weekend (Matt. 27:64 and 28:12, 13). It totally undermines the honesty and integrity of the disciples. Peter at Pentecost said, 'You put him to death by nailing him to the Cross. But *God raised him from the dead*' (Acts 2:23, 24). How could Peter, the former coward and one who denied Jesus, *now* psychologically, let alone morally make such a claim if the body of Jesus was mouldering in some hidden tomb, watched over by frightened disciples and sorrowing women?

Unless the sheer historical miracle that God raised Jesus from the dead on the third day took place our Gospel is false, the Apostles were liars, the New Testament is untrue, and the Church has been built on a lie for all these centuries.

Secondly, I recognise the honesty of the Bishop of Durham when he says in his Diocesan Newsletter, 'I cannot conceal or cheat on this because the whole matter is too important for cheating or concealment or pretending to particular beliefs that one does not find sufficient reason for holding.' (See p. 99.)

But if he is reported correctly, and if these are his considered views, and if he cannot unreservedly preach this Easter weekend that Jesus was raised on the third day, according to the Scriptures, then sadly I believe he should resign his bishopric and return to his academic work. (See p. 100.)

Above all else a bishop is called to be 'the guardian of the Christian faith' and with humble assurance and joy to proclaim the Easter message summed up in churches all over Christendom this weekend when we say:

> Christ has died
> Christ is risen
> Christ will come again.
> Alleluia!"

Are these issues of faith and doubt of such importance that they should be carefully and systematically discussed in public, or should bishops keep silent? Clearly for myself, I would not have taken such an extreme stand, calling for the Bishop of Durham's resignation, unless I felt this so very strongly. As brother bishops all of us seek to support each other in as fraternal a way as possible, and especially older bishops seek to support new bishops in the first years of their episcopate.

My final reason for taking such an extreme step has in fact been reflected in the steady stream of letters I have been receiving. I have been surprised by their numbers. Over 300 have written with thankfulness. Over 70, and many most courteously, have explained why they feel my call for the bishop's resignation was misconceived. I am heartened by those who have been helped by Dr. Jenkins' approach. I like him as a person and I wish him no harm.

Nonetheless, one letter stays in my mind, and I quote it, because I believe it truly reflects the seriousness of the present situation in the Church of England, when the Archbishop of York can speak of a "hierarchy of truth" to be believed in the debate on doctrine in the General Synod in February 1985, in which he is quoted as having "an open mind" about miracles. Another diocesan bishop uses the same phrase of "an open mind" about the doctrine of the Virgin Birth.

A former moderator of the Church of Scotland wrote to me saying:

What David Jenkins says is fearfully damaging to the Church, for 1) his statements about the faith are prevarications: he uses traditional language to say something very different; and 2) to say that Christ was not risen in body, and that someone stole away the body from the tomb, perhaps the disciples themselves, is to make the Apostolic Foundation of the Church rest on a deceit and a lie. He claims to be speaking for the Christian faith in a way that he thinks he must within a world of science – but he could not be more mistaken. Any scientific statement requires space-time coordinates, and any doctrine without coordinates in space and time is scientifically meaningless – empirical correlates are essential. But that is what the empty tomb is, for it means that the Resurrection is an act of God within space and time, within our physical world where we belong – otherwise the act of God is irrelevant to us who are physical as well as spiritual beings, and it is scientifically meaningless. The saving act of God certainly transcends the physical and historical, for it is an act of God, but it is an act of God within the physical structures of space and time where human beings belong and where God has put them. The Resurrection has to be looked at on two levels, on the level of space and time and on the level of the divine act, the former being open to the latter at what scientists call its "boundary conditions" and open to control or regulation

27

at that higher level. That makes the lower level all the more established as what it is. If David Jenkins is what St. Paul calls "a spiritual man", then he is not the less "man", because he is "spiritual" – likewise the "spiritual body" of the Resurrection is not less "body" because it is "spiritual" but all the more "body" for it has corruption and decay eliminated from it.

I do not enjoy controversy, and it is a temptation to spiritual pride to suggest others are wrong and one is right. Nevertheless, the events I am describing in the next chapter have been so heartwarming, and God is so wonderfully at work in so many hearts, and in recent months in so many local churches, that I want to make it clear that the Church of England at its heart is truly a believing Church. I affirm that it is led by believing bishops and is ready and eager to provide a warm welcome to all who are seeking and finding Christ today. This book is written to help doubters find faith, to help disciples to follow Christ more confidently, and to help those who are believers humbly and resolutely to share their faith with others, for I am sure "the gates of hell shall not prevail against the Church of Christ".

I return to the great truth of Christ's wonderful Resurrection more fully in Chapter 10.

2

"TELL OUT MY SOUL"

George Orwell's *1984* started on a Sunday. Bishops of Norwich by tradition are asked to preach on the first Sunday after Christmas at Sandringham Church, and are usually invited by the Queen to stay at Sandringham with the Royal Family for the weekend. As January 1st fell on a Sunday in 1984, it gave me the opportunity of looking forward into the New Year and of bringing a New Year message both to all inside our small Sandringham Church, and the 6,000 or 7,000 outside in the Park, who come to see the Royal Family drive or walk to church, and to join the Morning Service and listen to the sermon relayed to the Park.

First, I spoke about Mission England. Her Majesty had already invited Dr. Billy Graham to stay at Sandringham House a fortnight later. So in this same pulpit Billy Graham was about to preach on "Christ the Good Shepherd" and sharpen expectancy and promote prayer for this ambitious evangelistic project, leading to Dr. Graham's visit to the six football grounds in Bristol, Sunderland, Norwich, and then Birmingham, Liverpool and Ipswich. One million people heard his forthright and relevant proclamation of the Good News. 97,000 made some open response to Christ, but in addition, as we saw with great happiness in East Anglia, thousands of both young and mature Christians together with a broad spectrum of clergy – Anglican, Free Church and Roman Catholic – responded to practical training in the basics of Christian faith and service, and personal counselling in preparation for the six regional crusades.

Secondly, I spoke of 1984 as a year to remember our Christian heritage, because in May 1984 there was to be a great service in Westminster Abbey to commemorate the men and women of faith, throughout the long history of our nation, and to launch a year-long exploration along the Heritage Trails of our country. Many of our ancestors not only died for the Faith, but accomplished great things for God, and for society, and for the world, by such a firm grasp of the historic Christian Faith, that they put their faith to work for the good of their contemporaries, and those who would follow them. I remembered this four months later when I attended that historic service in Westminster Abbey, and saw again the words of William Carey, the great and humble missionary to Africa, who had been a cobbler, and said, "Expect great things from God. Attempt great things for God."

If God can take a cobbler like Carey, or a simple preacher like John Bunyan, or a quiet nun like Mother Teresa in our day, and use them to do great things for God, then if we can grasp the essential truths of the historic Christian Faith, set out in the Bible and taught down the years by the Church, perhaps God can release us and equip us and use us "in his service, which is perfect freedom", as the Prayer Book collect puts it.

When I preached that sermon in Sandringham Parish Church on the first day of 1984, I was not to know how wonderfully our prayers for Mission England were to be answered. Now at most Confirmations, in which one third of candidates are now over twenty-one years of age, and many of whom come in families, we are receiving many "Renewals of Baptism and Confirmation Promises" as the Norwich and Ipswich commitments become anchored in local church situations. Following Mission England in East Anglia 1,500 small nurture groups for Prayer and Bible Study, linked with local churches and chapels, have sprung up into new spiritual life.

My aim, therefore, is to provide a straightforward explanation of the Christian Faith, as it is rooted in history, set forth in the Bible, received down the centuries by the Church, and experienced today, as individually we respond in repentance and faith and obedience to Jesus Christ as our living Lord, and then grow up into him in the fellowship of his lively contemporary church.

Will you join me on this journey of exploration, where-ever you are in your present religious pilgrimage? In this next chapter, we go back about 570 years before St. Felix began to establish the church in East Anglia, for the Christian Church is stubbornly rooted in history. As the 110th Bishop of East Anglia, I feel quite a close affinity to our founding fathers, with St. Felix, and particularly, because my family has roots in the Celtic Church of St. Patrick, with St. Furzey of Ireland who established Christian work near Caister by Great Yarmouth in Norfolk. There have been 1,350 years of Christianity in East Anglia, and going back only about another 570 years further, we come to the Emperor Nero's persecution in Rome in AD 64.

3

"STRANGE VICTORY"

On our way home from leading a diocesan mission in
Gippsland, South Australia, my wife and I spent a
weekend in Rome, and visited the Catacombs, where
many of the early Christian martyrs were buried during
the savage persecutions under the Emperor Nero in AD 64.
If Christians were martyred for their faith, less than forty
years after Jesus died, and was raised from the dead by
God, their faith rested in that clearly attested fact. When
Paul wrote to the Corinthians in approximately AD 55 he
stated not only that "Christ died for our sins, according to
the Scriptures," but that "he was buried, and on the third
day" (as Jesus promised in his life (Mark 8:31)) "He rose
again, according to the Scriptures" (see 1 Corinthians
15:3–6). In his risen body, recognised by the nail-prints
in his hands, but transformed into his resurrection body
by which he could enter the closed doors of the Upper
Room, and showing himself to the disciples "as the first-
fruits from the dead", he brought them to full assurance
about his physical Resurrection.

Peter and the Twelve saw him, but so did "more than
500 brethren at one time, most of whom are still alive"
(AD 55) "but some are fallen asleep" (the beautiful phrase
that must have brought comfort to all post-Resurrection
Christians, whether dying by martyrdom five or ten years
later, or by natural causes).

Surely this means that those whose mortal remains were
the first to be laid in the Catacombs in Rome, and later
generations of Christians whose bodies were also laid

there, died not in a vague but forlorn hope that there might have been some "spiritual" resurrection of Jesus. They died in the knowledge that Peter's Pentecost sermon was demonstrably true, when preaching only walking distance from Joseph of Arimathea's open and empty tomb, he cried out "God raised him (Jesus) up, having loosed the pangs of death, because it was not possible for him to be held by it" (v. 24). The word "witness" in the Greek gives us our word "martyr" as well as "witness", in the English. The early martyrs under Emperor Nero's persecution died in the sure faith that death for the believing Christian was not the end: that Christ, who conquered death, gives life to us: that "the *last* enemy to be destroyed is death" in Paul's vivid phrase (1 Corinthians 15:26) and therefore "just as we have borne the image of the man of dust, we shall also bear the image of the man of heaven" (v. 49).

Will you read for yourself the "classic passage" in the Bible on the Resurrection in 1 Corinthians 15, to which we will return later in Chapter 4 when we work more fully at the miracle of the Resurrection? (See also Chapter 10.)

There is nothing proud, or self-opiniated, or obscurantist in believing whole-heartedly in the miraculous events of Easter Day. This was the concerted public witness of the eleven Apostles, once Thomas came to faith, a week after Easter Day (John 20:28–31). When Matthias had been chosen to replace Judas Iscariot, it was on the very grounds of being able to join the others by saying "We have seen the Lord," because an Apostle had to be a witness to the Resurrection:

"For it is written in the Book of Psalms, 'Let his habitation be desolate, and let no man dwell there in, and his bishopric let another take.' Wherefore of these men which have companied with us all the time that the Lord Jesus went in and out among us, beginning from the baptism of John, unto that same day that He was taken up from us, must one be ordained to be a witness with us of His resurrection . . . and Matthias was numbered with the eleven apostles" (Acts 1:20–26 AV).

I have copied this quotation out from the small pocket Bible in the Authorised Version, which was given me on my twentieth birthday, August 26th, 1936, and which I carried with me throughout the Second World War. It always reminds me of the inner assurance of eternal life, through trusting Christ as my personal Saviour, which I knew then as now. I also remember, with similar assurance, pointing my sailors and Royal Marines and other service men and women to Jesus Christ as Saviour and Lord, often under extreme conditions of danger.

I could not have done that, if I had not been sure that Christ had forgiven my sins, and had already given me his gift of eternal life, through faith in him. I believe the events of his death, and his burial, and his Resurrection from the empty tomb, really happened on those three days that changed the world. I believe that the statements of Christ were true, when he constantly prepared his disciples for the future.

"And He began to teach them that the Son of man must suffer many things, and be rejected by the elders, and the chief priests and the scribes, and be killed *and after three days rise again*" (Mark 8:31–32).

I believe that the New Testament accounts of Easter, even with their occasional and rough-hewn seeming discrepancies, which the early Church made no attempt to tidy up, or brush away, have such a ring of truth about them, that they can be accepted with assurance, and proclaimed today with whole-heartedness.

The B.B.C., in the fortieth anniversary year of D-Day, flew me back to the Normandy beaches where I had landed on that day, and drove me to the Cathedral at Bayeux, and to the Commonwealth Graves Commission Cemetery at Hermanville, which with two other chaplains I had first set up in the immediate aftermath of the landings on June 6th, 1944.

The B.B.C. programme was for immediate use on Remembrance Sunday, and as I walked through the quiet garden which had been a small orchard with wild dog-roses in its hedges, I found the permanent memorials of the young sailors, and Royal Marines and soldiers and airmen I had buried.

If I had not then believed fully in the historic fact that Christ died for our sins and in the miracle, "That He was raised on the third day, according to the Scriptures" (1 Corinthians 15:4), I could not have said the great words of the Prayer Book service time and time again:

> For as much as it hath pleased Almighty God of His great mercy to take unto Himself the soul of our dear brother here departed, we therefore commit his body to the ground; earth to earth, ashes to ashes, dust to dust; in sure and certain hope of the Resurrection to eternal life, through our Lord Jesus Christ; who shall change our (lowly) body, that it may be like unto His glorious body, according to the mighty working, whereby He is able to subdue all things to Himself.

We shall return to the central truth of Christ's death and Resurrection in more detail in Chapter 10 but for the moment I want clearly to affirm my personal belief in the Gospel records of Christ's Resurrection in bodily form on the third day. It is not a matter of academic or esoteric argument, but rather it is at the centre of the message we proclaim, and it is the sure comfort in sorrow we can offer to those who, however feebly and fearfully, stretch up their hand of faith to the nail-pierced but powerful hand of Jesus Christ, the conqueror of death.

This experience of trusting Christ is the valid testimony which Christians can give, from the Catacombs of the first century to the cemeteries of the twentieth century and all the centuries between. But who was, and who is, the one in whom Christians have believed throughout these days? In the next chapter we will go a little further into the Catacombs to find answers at a deeper level.

4

"JESUS IS LORD"

(An early credal statement of the Early Christians, found
in 1 Corinthians 12:3 following 1 Cor. 8:4–6)

The sheer size and depths of the Catacombs surprise you
on your first visit. As my wife and I traversed the various
galleries on a Sunday afternoon, the affirmation of the
primitive faith "Jesus is Lord" came to us, down the
centuries. And the almost crude drawings of Christ sitting
at the Holy Table with his disciples reminded me that first
in Jerusalem and later in Asia Minor, and finally in Rome,
the earliest Christians of Jewish stock moved the Sabbath
day of rest to the first day of the week for worship, because
on that first day of the week, Christ rose from the dead.

How could that frightened band of scattered Apostles
gather again at the Maundy Thursday instituted "Last
Supper" of the Lord, if he was dead? How could they bear
to break bread, in their sorrow, if they had stolen his
broken body from the tomb, before Easter morning? How
could they drink wine, when the blood from hands and
feet, from his brow and his side was dried brown on his
dead body in the tomb?

On the simplest psychological grounds the Apostles
could not have obeyed their Master's last command when
he had said "Do this in remembrance of ME" if their
memories stopped short at an empty cross and a closed
tomb, where his dead body lay, every time they came
together for the new service of Holy Communion, based
on the Passover meal.

Yet my most vivid memory of the Catacombs is the secret sign of the early Christians – which Christians are using over the world today.

I have met recently a Ugandan policeman, a Salvation Army officer in Hong Kong, an English youngster with (to me!) a strange hairstyle, a Member of Parliament; often in our own diocese of Norwich, I have had fellowship with brother and sister Christians "at the sign of the Fish".

In the Catacombs, it stands not only as a secret sign whereby Christians recognise each other, but as a witness to the faith of Christians living and dead, and remains so the world over to this day. The Greek word for fish is ICHTHUS, which is an acrostic:

JESUS	in Greek:	Iesous
CHRIST,		CHristos
OF GOD THE SON,		THeou
SAVIOUR		HUios
		Soter

If "Jesus is Lord" was the first passport within the fellowship whereby Christians recognised that people could only make that confession "by the Spirit" (1 Corinthians 12:3), "the Fish sign" is more, it is a primitive credal statement about who this man Jesus is, and who his followers, even to the death, maintain in their bold witness he truly is.

In this chapter, therefore, we must explore what the Fish sign really says, and then see if it is an authentic reflection of the slow, steady teaching of Jesus, in the days of his flesh. For Jesus wanted his inner circles, the Three, the Twelve, the Women who journeyed with the apostolic band, and the Seventy, slowly and steadily to understand who he really was, and is. So we will unpack the word Ichthus, which is one of the primitive symbols of the truth.

Jesus

Here is Jesus the human person. Jesus, "one of us" in our naming and our individuality and our person-hood! The name from the Old Testament means "Joshua" the young victorious leader, who led the children of Israel up to the Promised Land, and his name means Deliverer.

Christ

Here is the Messiah, the Anointed One, not only the Servant of Isaiah's prophecies, but the Suffering Servant, of whom the Old Testament prophesied.

Of God the Son

Here is the Divine title, not only Mary's baby boy, born in the obscurity and poverty of the Bethlehem cattle shed, but the very Son of God, from Eternity to Eternity. And now we are moving into the realm of defined theology. For the moment, listen to the Church of England's theological summary in Article 2 of the 39 Articles of Religion, to which every clergyman, when he becomes deacon, priest or bishop gives assent, before his ordination or consecration in a public and solemn statement, entitled "The Declaration of Assent" which he then signs and his bishop countersigns. In this way the Church of England maintains its general but gentle discipline.

Article 2 "Of the Word, or Son of God, which was made very Man" – "The Son, which is the Word of the Father, begotten from everlasting of the Father, the very and eternal God, and of one substance with the Father, took Man's nature in the womb of the Blessed Virgin of her substance . . ."

Saviour

The Name of Jesus, with its original Old Testament connotation of Deliverer, is now in Jesus revealed as the sinbearer and the Saviour, and is further amplified by the fuller but still very early, detailed and carefully handed-down credal statement of Paul.

We know more about the personality of Paul than most other Apostles, save for Peter. Paul was courageous, impulsive, "a loner", something of a Christian controversialist, yet gentle, easily hurt, but with a burning desire to proclaim the fulness of Christ's gospel to Jew and Gentile alike.

He places himself humbly in the central stream of the apostolic testimony and speaks of "what I received" and he can only be speaking of James, of Peter, of the leaders of the Church in Jerusalem, near the Upper Room, the Open Tomb and the Empty Cross, where the Church began.

Paul wrote his first letter to the Corinthians (who frankly were an impetuous and troublesome lot) in about AD 55, a mere twenty-five years after the events of the first Easter. He goes further. He says he has "received"; already this Good News "is of first importance". Here we are talking about a twenty-year time span, *half* the time between D-Day in 1944, a day that my generation still remembers with the events etched painfully and vividly on our memories, and the fortieth anniversary of June 1984.

Paul is not speaking of vague spiritual experiences, half-remembered in the mists of time. Here, surely, is the authentic and historic witness of the Apostles, soon to be set out in the Gospel narratives. It is recorded by the careful historian Luke in the Acts, with his painter's sense, and his medical understanding, when he chronicles Peter's Pentecost sermon (Acts 2:14–42) and its immediate results (vv. 43–47).

If you are finding faith difficult, or the variety of religious voices confusing, or your religious experience falling short of Thomas' testimony "My Lord and my God", when finally he broke through the dark barrier of doubt on the next Sunday evening after Easter (John 20:24–31), then may I recommend that you study 1 Corinthians 15:1–11.

The Apostolic Summary

"For I delivered to you as of first importance, what I also received, that Christ died for our sins in accordance with the Scriptures (and) that he was buried . . ." 1 Cor 15:3–4. It really happened. He truly died. The purpose was not just to show us love, which he most wonderfully did, but to bear our sins, their weight, their penalty, their rebellion against God and their cruelty to our fellow men. This was not a martyr's death, but the death of a sacrifice. Remember this was not just Mary's Son in his human nature, but the Divine and unique Son of God, bearing the sins of all humanity. No wonder Paul said that in his letter to the Corinthians this "was of first importance".

The second Article of the 39 Articles continues: "He truly suffered, was crucified, dead and buried, to reconcile his Father to us, and to be a sacrifice, not only for original guilt, but also for all actual sins of men."

Clearly Paul speaks of acts in human history, and a place in geography, when he states that "Christ died . . . and was buried". The burial, you remember, was in Joseph of Arimathea's new tomb, and the stone was rolled down into its socket and the seal was placed over the doorway and the soldiers settled down on watch.

Writing in *The Times*, Dr. John Scott argued that:

The Resurrection was a divine act of vindication. Moreover, since the verdict had been public, its reversal needed to be public too.

It was also historical, for it happened "on the third day". This apparently insignificant detail was part of the gospel which Paul said he had received and passed on to the others. It later became incorporated in the Apostles' Creed ("on the third day he rose again").

It bears witness to a dated event, and makes me wonder how Dr. David Jenkins in the now famous *Credo* television programme could have said that, even from reading Paul in 1 Corinthians, it did not seem to him that "there was any one event which you could identify with the Resurrection – only a series of experiences."

Experiences there certainly were, lasting forty days, but the event which gave rise to them happened on the third day.

Surely the Apostolic Summary rings true? The former Archbishop of Canterbury, Michael Ramsey, sums it up well, when he writes about Jesus in history and discusses "form" criticism (in *God, Christ and the World*). He finishes a closely reasoned argument by saying:

"The entire theme of this chapter would, however, collapse were it not for the Resurrection of Jesus. Without the Resurrection, the Christian movement would have petered out in ignomy and there would have been no Christianity. It is not too much to say that without the Resurrection, the phenomenon of Christianity in the apostolic age and since, is scientifically unaccountable. . . . The distinctiveness of Christianity is not its adherence to a teacher who lived long ago, but its belief that 'Jesus is Lord', for every generation through centuries.

"The Resurrection is something which 'happened' a few days after the death of Jesus. The Apostles became convinced that Jesus was alive, and that God had raised him to life. It is not historically scientific to say only that the Apostles came to realise the divine meaning of the crucifixion for them, or that the person of Jesus now became contagious to them.

"Something *happened* so as to vindicate for them the meaning of the Cross, and to make the person of Jesus contagious to them. The evidence for a stupendous happening, which the New Testament writers mention, was the *survival* of the Church, the appearances of Jesus in a visible and audible impact on the Apostles, and the discovery that the tomb was empty . . . As to significance, if it were the existential encounter of Jesus which alone mattered, then the empty tomb would have little or no significance. If, however, Jesus has a *cosmic* meaning with cosmic effects then the empty tomb has great significance, akin to the significance of the Incarnation itself . . . The Apostles, for all the existential character of the Easter faith, were yet at pains to confirm to themselves and others, that it was a reasonable faith, and that there were facts *inexplicable* apart from the Resurrection."

There, with the cautious and scholarly and faith-arousing words of the former archbishop, we see the Resurrection. We marvel at the courage and testimony of the early Christians whose symbols and words of faith still illumine the Catacombs of Rome, and in our pilgrimage we must now study Jesus, "His Godhead and Manhood, joined in One Person, never to be divided, whereof is one Christ, very God and very Man" (Article 2).

If this daunts you, we shall take this next stage of our pilgrimage of faith, not from the standpoint of the doctrinal formularies which the Church in the Articles and Creed seeks to promulge, in order that truth can be vividly taught and heresy boldly rebuked. Rather in this next stage we shall see how these wonderful events about the birth and life and ministry of Jesus impressed themselves upon Mary, his mother, and the early disciples.

5

GOD BREAKS IN

We now come to the best-known religious event in the
world – Christmas! Every opinion poll puts the basic
knowledge of Christmas at the top of the ratings, with
the basic knowledge of Easter lower down, and as the
sports commentators love to say, with Whit Sunday
"trailing".

It would be impossible to look in the window of a large
store in December each year anywhere in the Western
world, without seeing some sign of the birth of the baby
Jesus. It would be impossible not to hear Christmas carols
on the radio, and particularly Martin Luther's famous
children's carol:

> Away in a manger,
> No crib for a bed,
> The little Lord Jesus
> Laid down his sweet head.

At this point we come up against the stubborn fact that
the church's Handbook claims that at a place in geography,
the small royal city of Bethlehem, and at a moment in
history (Luke the cautious historian says "in the days of
Caesar Augustus and when Quirinius was Governor of
Syria . . ." Luke 2:1, 2) a baby called Jesus was born. *That
is an historical fact of such widespread acceptance* that
faith is not needed to believe it to be true. Even the
Government of the USSR, with its atheistic department
to deal with religion and curtail freedom of religious

instruction and witness, finds itself speaking of AD 1985, Anno Domini, the year of the Lord.

Here comes the complementary question. How was the baby born, and who really is he?

A Special Entrance

Having established the fact of his birth, if we are to move forward to a reasonable faith, we must ask questions about the "How", "Who" and "Why" of his birth.

When my wife Margaret and myself first went to the Holy Land a number of years ago we came to Bethlehem and the Grotto of the Nativity. There the lamps flickered, the absorbed reverent faces of kneeling Orthodox nuns, seemed carved, Dürer-like, out of pale oak, and all was still. And we too knelt and remembered in prayer and gratitude that "Away in a Manger" two thousand years ago Jesus was born.

When we were home again, we described the Grotto of the Nativity, the traditional site of the Manger, to Jane who was then five years old. Her little eyes lit up, and she said "and was the *hay* still there?" The imagination of a child can bridge twenty centuries, and must not be despised. Our Lord himself "took the small children into his arms, and blessed them, laying his hands upon them", and said "Let the children come to me, do not hinder them; for to such belongs God's Kingdom. Truly I say to you, whoever does not receive the Kingdom of God like a child shall not enter it" (Mark 10: vv. 16, 14 and 15.)

As a bishop and a guardian of the Faith by virtue of my office, I have a responsibility to put as simply as I can the sheer historic fact of the birth of the baby Jesus, and then as clearly and positively as I can, to explain the immense range of truths that stem from the questions: how did he come? Why was he sent? Who was he?

The Christian Faith teaches (and I believe) that God who created his world, by the activity of his eternal Son, now in the Person of his Son and by the action of the Third

Person of the Trinity, the Holy Spirit, was conceived in the womb of the Virgin Mary, and was made man and was born in the stable beneath the Inn at Bethlehem – that is breath-taking, but I believe, TRUE!

Read the account of creation in Paul's letter to the Colossians, in one of the richest Christological passages in the Bible:

> . . . giving thanks to the Father, who has qualified us to share in the inheritance of the saints in light. He has delivered us from the dominion of darkness and transferred us to the kingdom of his beloved Son, in whom we have redemption, the forgiveness of sins. *He is the image of the invisible God*, the first-born of all creation; for in him all things were created, in heaven and on earth, visible and invisible, whether thrones or dominions or principalities or authorities – all things were created through him and for him. *He is before all things, and in him all things hold together*. He is the head of the body, the church; he is the beginning, *the first-born from the dead*, that in everything he might be pre-eminent. For in him all the fulness of God was pleased to dwell (Colossians 1:12–19).

If this is the quality of the Baby who was born on that cold Christmas night, surely we would expect the miraculous to be inextricably bound up with him. For a miracle at its simplest, means that God, who created our world, and who planned the natural laws by which our world coheres and consistently continues (as Paul said to the doubting and even mocking Athenians on Mars Hill), is the God who "himself gives to all men life and breath and everything" (Acts 17:25). He now breaks into his ordered laws with a higher law of sovereign and Divine action in his Son, and for our highest good. His coming was not wholly unexpected, because God's continuous activities chronicled in the Old Testament show his constant concern for his creatures. The Ten Commandments are not cruel inhibitions, but loving signposts to warn, to check, to enlighten and so to guide us into the path of God's best purposes for our lives. The code of sacrifices for sins, leading up to the Day of Atonement and the Passover meal, are not designed to depress God's people with a sense of guilt, but through the shed blood of the victim, to release his people into the freedom of forgiveness, and towards the peace of pardon.

The message of the prophets was not only condemnatory, by arousing a sense of sin and the moral understanding of transgression, but the prophets pointed forward to God's Kingdom of Truth and righteousness and the coming of the Suffering Servant of Jehovah, who was to be the Christ, the Sin-bearer, the Lord.

The mature men and women of faith were not surprised, but only joyful when Jesus was born. For example, Simeon was "looking for the consolation of Israel" and Anna was another (Luke 2:25). "It had been revealed to Simeon by the Holy Spirit, that he should not see death, before he had seen the Lord's Christ (v. 26)."

In other words God's stage-hands had been patiently setting the stage of history, for his Coming One, and the prologue to the drama promised a special entrance and a unique character, as prophesied in the Old Testament.

The Unique Character

Old Testament prophecy had an immediate purpose, but also a Messianic promise, and we can see this clearly from the post-Resurrection Church, and we can be strengthened in our present faith, by these prophecies of the past. Hebrews 11 relates to this. Four references will suffice to show the direction of our research.

1. God's revelation of himself as the eternal, ever-present "I AM" used as the Divine Name. In the seven great declarations of Jesus in John's Gospel, he claims the Divine title, as in "I AM the way, the truth and the life, no man comes to the Father but by me" (John 14:6).

2. The Passover Lamb. See Exodus 12:1–14 and Mark 14:12–28, where Jesus clearly likens himself to the Lamb,

whereby the Israelites in Egypt received deliverance, and claims to fulfil the Zechariah 13:7 prophecy of the suffering Shepherd for Himself.

3. The Suffering Servant, and later the Messiah, the Anointed One, who dies for the sin of the people (*see* Isaiah 53:3–12 and Luke 22:37) when under the very shadow of Calvary on the following day, Jesus speaks of the Isaiah prophecy being fulfilled in Himself.

4. The Christ, the Son of God. See the great names of Deity, linked with the Messiah who would come to us. It is difficult even to read the names without hearing Handel's majestic music in *Messiah* undergirding the prophetic titles. (*See* Isaiah 9:6–7.)

I share these prophecies with you, reinforced as true to the unique character of the Messiah to be born in Bethlehem, because Jesus himself refers to them in his early ministry, to show that it will not do, if we are to be orthodox believing Christians, to emphasise only the humanity of Mary's baby boy. The Bible claims and Christ explains and the Church proclaims that the unique Person who was born to the Virgin Mary was none other than God incarnate.

We are now unavoidably involved in miracle: i.e., God's own sovereign choice of the special way in which his Son was to take human flesh. We cannot side-step this issue, because not only do bishops at their ordination openly and whole-heartedly express their faith, through the Nicene Creed just before they are consecrated, but when they ordain deacons and priests to the sacred ministry, they publicly examine them concerning their belief in the Scriptures and the expression of that faith in the Creeds. We assert:

I believe in Jesus Christ, his only Son, our Lord.
He was conceived by the power of the Holy Spirit
    and born of the Virgin Mary,
He suffered under Pontius Pilate,
    was crucified, died, and was buried.
He descended to the dead.

On the third day he rose again.
He ascended into heaven,
    and is seated at the right hand of the Father.
He will come again to judge the living and the dead.

For the Church to ask such whole-hearted affirmations of
the Faith, at this most solemn moment of our ministerial
lives, is not to put us clergy into intellectual blinkers.
Nobody forces us to be ordained, but the Church has the
right to invite her ministers to assent openly to the basic
historic facts of the Christian Faith, centring in the birth,
life, death, resurrection and ascension of the Lord Jesus
Christ. The Church of England is a Catholic church in its
tradition and a Reformed church in its dependence on the
Bible.

On Trinity Sunday, in the year I am writing this book,
I shall complete forty-five years as a parson, as deacon, as
priest and fourteen years as bishop. My own testimony is
not very startling, but in days which are confusing for
faith, I give it. For forty-five years I have been glad to say:

I bind unto myself this day,
the strong Name of the Trinity.

I have found the love of God our heavenly Father, the
salvation and living friendship of Jesus Christ our Lord,
and the enlightenment and freshness of God the Holy
Spirit, the very mainspring of my daily life. I find the
gentle discipline of the Church of England, inviting me to
believe no more than Holy Scriptures clearly teaches,
together with such teaching of the Creeds and Ancient
Fathers of the Church as are agreeable to the same, leads
me forward into broad pastures; as broad and deep as the
love of God is for all his children.

I find no restriction of intellect, or conflict of scientific
theory, as I share with you my belief in the first of the
procession of miracles, which are the very hallmarks of
the life of Jesus Christ our Lord on earth. So we study
together "the doctrine of the Virgin Birth" or as the

present Bishop of London in his recent and refreshing book *Firmly I Believe and Truly*, calls it, "the Virginal Conception".

Christian doctrines are not accepted because they can be mathematically proved, and each of us must unpack our own suppositions, which we call insights and those who think differently from us might call prejudices.

I admit my suppositions, and share them with you.

I believe in God's use of miracle, and I also recognise that miracles in, say, John's Gospel are also stated to be signs (see Chapter 11 on A Reasonable Faith in Miracles).

I believe in the authority of Old and New Testament, as God by his Holy Spirit inbreathes the large number of human authors in their diversity, and without stifling their human minds, equips them to reveal the truth of God, in various but harmonious ways, so that we can talk not only about a library of 66 books, but about the Bible as one Book. So I recognise miracles may well be promised and may happen in Scripture. (See Chapter 9 on the authority of the Bible.)

I believe that such a wholly unique event as the sending by God of his eternal Son to live as Man amongst us, would most likely come about in an equally unique fashion, and so I am pre-disposed to accept this particular event of the Virginal Conception of our Lord, as (a) probable, (b) as likely to be fully recorded in Scripture and (c) as congruous.

6

"O COME, O COME, EMMANUEL . . ."

*(The Testimony
of Matthew)*

The statements about the Virgin Birth

Certainly there is plenty of Bible material. Earlier in this
book we have seen how Old Testament types and pictures
and prophecies look forward to such an event. Jesus himself tells a story about a distant King steadily and patiently
desiring to bring his rebel subjects back to loyal obedience
and loving service. When other actions seem ineffective,
the King acts decisively: "Afterward he sent his son to
them, saying 'They will *respect* my son,' but when the
tenants saw the son, they said to themselves, 'This is the
heir; come, let us kill him and have his inheritance . . .'
When the chief priests and pharisees heard his parables,
they perceived that he was speaking about them. But
when they tried to arrest him, they feared the multitudes,
because they held Jesus to be a prophet" (Matt. 21:37–38,
45–46).

In effect, Jesus confirms the Old Testament prophecies
that God's Son would come among us. Isaiah 7:10–15 is
the best known "proof text" and Biblical critics tend not
to accept its validity, by not accepting it as prophecy, by
saying that "Virgin" can mean just "young girl", and by
relating it so firmly to Ahaz's day, that they do not accept
its wider Messianic significance. Against that, Christ himself recognises and validates the principle of prophecy
in Isaiah; Matthew boldly asserts that this prophecy is
directly fulfilled, following the angel of the Lord's clear

statement of the Virginal Conception to Joseph, when he discovered to his dismay that the Virgin Mary was "found to be with child" (v. 18) – see Matthew 1:22, 23. Thirdly, the critics are left with the necessity of explaining the prophecy of "Emmanuel" (Isaiah 7:14), the translation of Emmanuel as "God with us" in Matthew 1:23, and the obvious inference that Isaiah's prophecy, fulfilled in Matthew, and the message of the angel, point unitedly not only to a special and miraculous conception, to the assurance that this Virgin Birth is known and planned by God through the Holy Spirit, but also that the one who is so to be miraculously conceived, and uniquely born, is "Emmanuel – God with us."

I find this so cumulatively powerful, that I would find it harder to disbelieve than to believe in the Virginal Conception, as the Scriptures tell it, and as the Church down the centuries in the Creeds has proclaimed it.

The events portrayed in Matthew's Gospel

The three Synoptic Gospels of Matthew, Mark, and Luke, give a complementary picture of the life of Jesus. They are written from different viewpoints, and the background and personality of the three human authors, orchestrated to a harmony by the Holy Spirit, the Divine author, provide us with a "3-D" view, which one solitary narrative would not give. Mark, a young man in a hurry, and relying strongly on material from Peter, goes straight into the early ministry of Jesus, from the time of his baptism by John the Baptist (Mark 1:1–11) and tells us nothing of the events of Jesus' birth twenty-eight or thirty years before, nor does he record John's birth.

Similarly, John's Gospel, after the sublime start (John 1:1–14) of the traditional Christmas Gospel of the Eucharist, concerning the Light of the World, goes straight to our Lord's public ministry, heralded by John the Baptist in a detailed form not dissimilar from Mark.

But first we study the short, rather factually reported description, in Matthew. Those who find that the Virgin

Birth leaves them "with an open mind", sometimes suggest on these and other truths that there are different "genres" in the Bible, and that poetry, myth, parable, and fact, can be confused. There is no chance of confusing myth with fact in Matthew, chapter 1. Matthew begins by placing the birth of Jesus fairly and squarely within the long genealogical line of the Jewish people (v. 1). "The book of the genealogy of Jesus the Christ, the son of David, the son of Abraham." First, Matthew traces the family in which Jesus is to be brought up through Joseph's line. The outside contemporary world would think of him in these terms: "Is not this Joseph's son?" they would say, not knowing the mystery of the Virgin Birth (see Luke 4:22).

Secondly, it is within the constraints of Joseph's family, into which Jesus was to be born, that the journey to Bethlehem from the carpenter's shop at Nazareth had, perforce, to be embarked upon: "And Joseph also went up from Galilee, from the city of Nazareth, to Judea, to the city of David, which is called Bethlehem, because he was of the house and lineage of David, to be enrolled with Mary, his betrothed, who was with child" (Luke 2:4, 5).

Thirdly, Matthew bluntly ends the saga of the family tree, by stating bluntly, ". . . Jacob the father of Joseph the husband of Mary, of whom Jesus was born, who was called Christ." Having established with an almost clinical precision the fact that Jesus came in his humanity into our world, by human birth and that he was the Messiah, Matthew states bluntly: "Now the birth of Jesus the Christ took place *in this way*." Then compressed into eight short verses, without embroidery, or excuse, or hyperbole, Matthew succinctly states the truths around the miraculous conception and subsequent human birth to the Virgin Mary, of the baby Jesus. What are these clusters of truths, close knit together, so that the Bible presents us with an "all or nothing situation", and which the Church from its early creeds proclaimed to be true, and reverently, worthy of belief?

(v. 18) 1. Joseph and Mary were betrothed, but not married.

(v. 18) 2. Before they were married, Mary "was found to be with child".

(v. 18) 3. The child was "of the Holy Spirit", and not of human generation ("before they came together").

(v. 19) 4. Joseph's natural shock, and distress, caused him, "for he was a just and also compassionate man", to plan "to divorce her quietly".

(v. 20) 5. Before he did this, an angel messenger of the Lord, while he slept, broke into his troubled dreams, with this startling word: "Joseph, son of David, do not fear to take Mary your wife, for that which is conceived in her is of the Holy Spirit." The child was to be brought up in "a son of David's home", who would care for and protect mother and baby. The baby's conception was by a miracle, and the baby's birth was to be through the gateway of human birth: "she will bear a son" (v. 21).

(v. 21) 6. The son will be called JESUS, the Old Testament name of Joshua, the brave young warrior, the Deliverer, who led his people up to victory. This Jesus will be the Saviour deliverer, who will save his people from their sins, in an even greater deliverance.

(v. 24, 25) 7. Joseph woke, and obeyed the angel messenger of the Lord, and the account ends by the prosaic statement that "Joseph knew her not until she had borne a son", and in obedience to the Divine Word, Joseph called his name JESUS.

Matthew writes tersely, factually and from a strong Jewish standpoint, with the genealogies as the framework, and four Old Testament prophecies in support, in his first two chapters. Joseph is the most sharply etched character of the three, and once he has established the miracle of the Virginal Conception, he moves on to write of Herod, the Wise Men and the flight into Egypt. I get the feel of a man-to-man encounter. The no-nonsense converted chief tax collector talks with the chief carpenter of Nazareth.

A digression on believing

Before we go further, we need to remember, however, that Christ does not overwhelm us *emotionally* at the sight of his Cross, although he says: "I, when I am lifted up from the earth, will draw all men to myself. He said this to show what death he was to die" (John 12:32, 33). Neither does he overwhelm us *intellectually*, by placing the truths of the Faith before our minds so convincingly that reluctantly we *must* believe. Still we say, "Lord I believe, help thou my unbelief." Neither does he override our *wills*, because he looks for responsive disciples, not men and women pressed by Church or family or society into a religious conformity. He says, "*If any man* would come after me, let him deny himself and take up his cross *daily* and follow *me*" (Luke 9:23).

Yet a number of the letters I have received this year suggest that people have sadly come to a standstill about faith, and are crippled on their pilgrimage by doubts. If at times the modern Church seems to lack conviction, they suggest, perhaps we must come to terms with our doubts. Not so! There is nothing religiously meritorious in living in a twilight state of doubt. Jesus loved to state openly: "I am the Light of the world: he who follows me will not walk in darkness, but will have the light of life" (John 8:12).

Nevertheless Christian Faith is different from the world's credulity. The world says, "Show me, and I will believe," but the demonstration of total mathematical certitude leads only to logical agreement. Faith is always an adventure, but based upon revealed truth, and depending also upon obedient response to the truth as it is at present perceived by us.

Before we leave this digression on general faith, let me share one clue with you, if, quite literally, you are like the two disciples of Jesus on their way to Emmaus, on the afternoon of Easter Day, before their eyes were opened to see him as their risen and conquering Saviour, risen that very day from the Open Tomb. "They stood still, looking sad" (Luke 24:17). If that phrase should accurately describe your own spiritual position, study Christ's words in John 7:16. The Jews "marvelled" that he was such an able teacher, "when he has never studied", presumably meaning that he had not studied in the Rabbinic schools. Jesus replied to them: "My teaching is not mine, but His, who sent me. If any man's will is to do His will, he shall know whether the teaching is from God, or whether I am speaking on my own authority" (v. 17). In other words, if we turn to Christ in obedience, he will reveal himself to our eyes of faith. In recent months, since our "Mission England" meetings with Dr. Billy Graham at Norwich and at Ipswich, in many parishes those already baptised and confirmed have, usually at new Confirmations, openly renewed their baptism and confirmation promises locally. I have been moved by the serious and sincere way people have responded to my question, "Do you turn to Christ?" as in obedience and faith they have replied, "I turn to Christ."

The promises of salvation are set out clearly in the new Confirmation Service. They are repentance from sin, and faith in Christ, leading to obedience. Paul summarised them when he declared the heart of the Gospel message to be proclaimed to Jew and Gentile alike was: "repentance towards God, and faith in our Lord Jesus Christ" (Acts 20:21).

As we now continue with the study of the doctrines surrounding the birth of Jesus, do not be despondent, and feel that until you fully understand and accept the doctrine of the Virgin Birth, you cannot be a proper Christian. We are disciples of Christ, always learning, which is what the word disciple means. But if we are to be assured, and to be Christians growing in the faith, then we need to grasp firmly, and make our own, those great truths which the Bible clearly teaches, and which the Church in its statements of faith gladly proclaims.

7

"THE ANGEL GABRIEL
FROM HEAVEN CAME . . ."

*(The Testimony
of Luke)*

When our eldest son, Andrew, was thirteen he was the leading treble in his junior school choir, and he had to sing the first verse of this chapter's carol at the school Christmas Carol Service, as a solo. He sang with such a clear and beautiful melodic line, that the school recorded it for us. Four years later at his senior school, now as a tenor, we again recorded his voice. For his twenty-first birthday, to his slight embarrassment, but to the great enjoyment of the family, we played both recordings, and the child's voice and the young man's voice were both complementary and pleasing, though the person was the same. The Christmas Story remains the same down the centuries. As we grow and mature, we can and should understand it at an ever deeper level – but we never grow *beyond* it. We simply grow in maturity of faith.

The events portrayed in Luke's Gospel

In the opening chapters of Luke (1:5–2:40) we have the fullest account of the birth narratives, of John, as well as Jesus.

Luke writes for Theophilus ("Lover of God" in Greek) and sets out his material for other Gentile believers, so that with Theophilus they may receive "an orderly account", so "that you may know the truth concerning the things of which you have been informed" (1:3, 4).

Clearly Luke writes many years later. There have been "other narratives" (1:1) he has learnt from, "eye-witnesses", and he has pondered "for some time past" the need to write. Here is the thoughtful physician, gathering together his case-notes, and starting to write an orderly chronicle of the life and work of Jesus. Tradition calls him an artist, even as we know he was a doctor, and clearly he received much of the birth narratives from Mary herself, who perhaps felt able to confide professionally as well as to talk personally with "the beloved physician". Let us now look at the text in detail.

(1) The fact of Mary's virginity and (only) her betrothal are established (1:27) as in Matthew 1:18.

(2) Gabriel, the angel messenger, appeared to her in Nazareth. Her fears were stilled (1:30) and then the full revelation was given to her.

(3) Mary the Virgin would conceive (1:31). The child was to be called Jesus (cf. the same name given to Joseph for the baby, Matt. 1:21) and he would be "the Son of the Highest" (1:32) and be seated for ever on David's throne, which would clearly show Mary that God had chosen her to be "the mother of my Lord", the Christ (1.33, 1:43).

(4) In an even more pronounced way than to Joseph in Matthew's Gospel, the sheer miracle of the Virginal Conception, by the Holy Spirit, is spelt out with deliberate clarity.

(5) "Therefore the child to be born will be called holy, the Son of God" (1:35).

(6) With great gentleness, Gabriel encourages her with the good news of her elderly kinswoman, Elizabeth, who was already six months along the road towards the birth of John the Baptist, whom Mary immediately went to visit (1:36–39).

(7) Mary gladly accepts this holy and awesome responsibility: "Behold, I am the handmaid of the Lord: let it be to me according to your Word" (1:38), and with his work done, "the angel departed from her" (1:38).

The Church is very down to earth. And as every human young mother waits for nine months from conception, to the birth of the child, so the Church dates Lady Day as March 25th, and so the Nativity of Our Lord is observed on December 25th.

The standard works on the 39 Articles by Bishop Gibson of Gloucester, Professor Bicknell of London University, Dr. Griffith Thomas of Wycliffe Hall and Professor of Theology in Toronto, and others, all note the various objections to belief in the doctrine of the Virgin Birth, and the old criticisms are still voiced every ten or twenty years, and again in our day. For instance, that Paul was silent. But Paul would have known the whole story from his friend and travelling companion and fellow worker, Luke. References in Galatians 4:4 to his birth, and in 1 Corinthians 15 to his manhood, suggest a knowledge, but a reticence.

This reticence is most clearly understood if we remember that Mary was alive, and engaged within our Lord's earthly ministry, and probably only a chosen few knew the whole story, during the short earthly life of Jesus, lasting 32 or 33 years.

The centre of the Gospel message related to Christ's life, death, and Resurrection. Only later did it become increasingly necessary for new generations of Christians in the apostolic and sub-apostolic age to know the full framework of the life of Jesus from the first miracle of his wonderful birth to the concluding miracle of his glorious Resurrection. Meanwhile he endured the occasional taunt of his enemies: "*We* were not born of fornication: *we* have one Father, even God" (John 8:41), for clearly there were rumours, during his earthly life.

For myself, the Scriptural record is so full and clear and cohesive, that I find myself approaching the credal statement, not "with an open mind", as some who doubt its truth put it, but with a joyful heart. Jesus is truly "one of us" in his humanity, and he entered our world through the common gateway of human birth. Yet, "this child shall be

called holy" (1:35), and the entail of original sin, which
each of us receive from our human parents, is broken for
him. From his birth, he is "son of Mary" in his humanity,
but never less than "Son of God" in his divinity. It took
the theologians a long time to define who he truly is, yet
the youngest child can stretch out the hand of faith to him
as Shepherd and Saviour, as Son of Man and Son of God.

How else could the Second Person of the Trinity, from
eternity to eternity, take human flesh? What other explanation but fornication could account for his earthly life, and
the blunt statement of the enemies' taunt shows us how
morally untenable would that thesis be?

At the end of these three chapters, we have come full
circle. We speak truth, when we say publicly in the Nicene
Creed:

> We believe in one Lord, Jesus Christ
> the only Son of God,
> eternally begotten of the Father,
> God from God, Light from Light
> true God from true God
> begotten, not made,
> of one Being with the Father.
> Through him all things were made.
> For us men and for our salvation
> he came down from heaven;
> by the power of the Holy Spirit
> he became incarnate of the Virgin Mary, and was
>   made man.
> For our sake he was crucified under Pontius Pilate;
> he suffered death and was buried.
> On the third day he rose again
> in accordance with the Scriptures;
> he ascended into heaven
> and is seated at the right hand of the Father.
> He will come again in glory
> to judge the living and the dead,
> and his kingdom will have no end.

In so attesting to his unique birth and holy life, we also attest to God's activity of miracle, and yet at the end of this story, we are surely led to say, "Miracle – yes? but such a natural, matter-of-fact miracle." If God breaks into his world, as we believe he did, should we not expect miracle, and rejoice in it, and join Mary, the mother of our Lord, that most lovely and lowly person by saying:

> My soul magnifies the Lord,
> and my spirit rejoices in God my Saviour.
> (Luke 1:46, 47)

8

"WHO IS THIS . . . ?"

*(Advent Hymn – from O come,
O come, Emmanuel)*

I have mentioned D-Day, on June 6th, 1944. I was a young chaplain of twenty-seven, with R. N. Beach Commandos, when I landed on D-Day near Ouistreham, on the extreme left of the British Assault, just north of Caen, before re-joining Royal Marines as chaplain to 48 R.M. Commando a month later. As I prayed with scores of wounded men both British and Canadian, as well as caring for French civilians and German prisoners, the memories of that one historic day remain etched on my mind, sharp and clear, forty years later with an indelible quality.

As a chaplain I carried no weapons, of course, for I was simply a clergyman doing my ordinary job of preaching, celebrating Holy Communion, bringing the knowledge of Christ to the dying, praying with the wounded, and cheering them as best I could, and steadying the men under fairly continuous fire. I was immensely strengthened to be working alongside the R.A.M.C. senior doctor on Sword Beach. He was a cheerful, sensible, and convinced Christian, and his spoken Christian witness, supported by his resolute professional doctoring, made a strong impact on our many wounded men. We got as many as possible of them into amphibious D.U.K.W.S. (or "Ducks"), and off the beach to the empty and returning landing craft. It was non-stop work, and on D+1, I had noted in my "Daily Light" book of Bible verses, that we got 862 wounded men back to England on that first full day.

Working amongst young Royal Marines of 18 and 19 years of age, in training camps, in the year before D-Day, many of whom had virtually no knowledge of the Christian Faith, I had each batch of new recruits for eight weeks. Where to begin? I got plenty of Mark's Gospels, and John's Gospels, as well as whole New Testaments from the Naval and Military Bible Society, each in blue covers with the gold Naval Crest embossed on the cover, so that the young men felt the Gospels really were meant for them.

The senior chaplain had those confirmed before joining, and those put, perhaps a little hastily, through Confirmation at the base camp at Lympstone near Exeter, where they had real hot and cold water, and it was rumoured, baths.

The training sergeant would march my sixty young men into my Nissen hut chapel, shout "Sit to attention," and when both hands were resting on both knees in a parallel and military way, and all eyes were to the front, he would quietly retire from the chapel for a smoke, and in this devotional atmosphere, I would begin to talk about the Christian religion to my captive audience of young non-volunteers. Once again, where to begin? I told them one clean, sure-fire, funny story, which though it got a bit threadbare to me, day after day, did the trick of establishing contact.

I then gave every man a copy of Mark's Gospel, and we went swiftly into action, because there are at least *eight* clear, succinct, dramatic stories about Jesus in the very first chapter. Slowly, stumblingly, carefully (it was only this year that the famous Butler Education Act (1944) which provided a daily Christian Assembly in every state school was passed), we read the stories out loud, together, as best we could.

Jesus, as a living Person, became vividly alive for us. And I realised how Mark, "the young man in a hurry", by God's gracious Spirit had written timeless pictures, and told arresting stories, that brought my very young Royal Marines, soon to encounter the extreme challenge of action, face to face with Jesus Christ, through whom alone we can "make our peace" with God. Young and inexperienced though I was as a clergyman, only ordained three or four years, I was discovering that the stories of the life and death and resurrection of Jesus Christ, clearly and simply taught from the Gospels, with illustrations from our daily life together in the Services, really gripped these young men.

In the fairly concentrated work of a training establishment, seeing men each week for Religious Instruction, each Sunday for church services, and on Wednesdays for a voluntary Bible Study, I was able regularly to present men for Confirmation at the end of their courses. I am afraid we chaplains worked the Bishop of Crediton, and sometimes the Bishop of Plymouth, and occasionally the Diocesan Bishop of Exeter himself, very hard in those days!

I give you this long introduction to this chapter on the person of Jesus to fire you with enthusiasm to study Mark's Gospel for yourself, or better still, in a group, because once you start, you are carried along by Mark's almost breathless haste, "immediately" (1:12), "immediately" (1:18), "immediately" (1:20), "immediately" (1:21), "immediately" (1:23). There is still an "at once" and two more "immediately's" in the first chapter, making eight in all!

Will you apply this to your own situation, or to your church, or house group, or home, or school? Nothing is more spiritually invigorating, or clarifying to either your own faith, or those for whom you may be responsible, than reading the actual narrative of the life of Jesus.

One of my brother bishops told me that he gave a young Liverpool teenager a lift in his car. After he had criticised all the churches strongly but cheerfully, he suddenly turned to the bishop, and said, "But JESUS – he's a LUVELY person," in pure and beautiful Scouse. If we are to share our faith with others, we have to recover our confidence in the sheer fact that Jesus draws people to himself, and it is our task to open the Bible, the written Word, and show people Jesus, the living Word of God.

This will mean not simply "naming the Name", and that we do not do enough. It will mean explaining who he is in all his fulness, and to do that, we will now take a close look at Mark's Gospel, and follow through two main lines of enquiry, which will deepen our understanding of the Gospel, and equip us better to share it with others.

English people are by nature pragmatic, rather than dialectical, and perhaps for this reason my week by week study of Mark's Gospel, strong on action, short on parable, compared with Matthew and Luke, appealed to their pragmatic minds.

Mark has a most modest twin-track aim, when he starts his short book with the sudden and striking words: "The beginning of the Gospel of Jesus Christ, the Son of God" (Mark 1:1).

Mark is concerned that we should understand who Jesus, here named the Christ, the Son of God, truly is. Secondly, he explains the purpose for which this Jesus came.

He sets out his arguments to demonstrate that Jesus is divine, in his Person, and has come to the world for our salvation, in his purpose, in the way that today a good documentary television programme would do it. That is, with clear, sharply etched, quickly changing images, building up layers of knowledge that lead honest seekers, with steadily dissolving doubts, to say openly and with humble assurance, "This man was the Son of God." This is what the tough Roman centurion, who had no doubt supervised many an earlier crucifixion, said when "he stood facing Jesus, as He breathed his last: 'This man was the Son of God'" (Mark 15:39).

Who is Jesus?
John the baptiser (1:4) prepares the way of the Lord, with a call to repentance, leading to God's forgiveness, and arouses the people to expect One greater than he, who

will baptise not with water, but by the Holy Spirit, and immediately Jesus receives water baptism by John "to fulfil all righteousness," comments Jesus in the Matthew account (Matt. 3:15) perhaps with the reminder that Jesus enters fully into the condition of humanity, being truly man, "yet without sin" (Heb. 4:15). John gives a fuller account, when he writes in later years, and expands on the significance of our Lord's baptism from heaven by the Holy Spirit (John 1:23–34) with John the Baptist's summary: "And I have seen and have borne witness that this is the Son of God" (John 1:34), whereas Mark allows the voice from Heaven to explain the fact of Jesus's divinity, without comment: "Thou art my beloved Son (or my Son, the Beloved One); with thee I am well pleased."

After the anointing of Jesus, as the Christ, and the fierce temptations in the wilderness which Jesus, in his humanity, had to suffer, though strengthened by the Spirit (1:12), Jesus enters his public ministry. Immediately he outlines the challenge to moral and intellectual belief inherent in "the Gospel of God" and calls for repentance and faith, leading to the challenge to our wills: "Follow me" (1:15, 17) to the first disciples.

The Church of England always stresses this threefold Gospel challenge to the individual, in its Baptism services (infant and adult), its Confirmation services (the Decision and the Profession of Faith) and its Catechism. Our revised Confirmation Service now makes this abundantly clear. When as a fifteen-year-old schoolboy I was confirmed in my school chapel, I only had to say publicly the two shortest words in the English language, when I was asked in the old Prayer Book service if "I would believe and do all that my godparents had undertaken for me." "I do," I replied.

When fifty years later, to the very date (such are the cheerful coincidences of God!), with the warm goodwill of the local diocesan bishop, I confirmed a number of boys in the same school chapel, I was glad that of all the various revised services in our Church (whether you yourself like them, or not!) I was able to use our present Confirmation

Service, and this lesson in Mark 1:14–20 is one of the suggested passages. Repent: Believe: Follow Christ – here are the central responses of the soul to God. They are claimed for us, on the faith of our parents and godparents, or sponsors. Here is the gateway, in its approach infinitely varied, in God's good planning, but through its archway, clearly necessary, for the soul to find its way, slowly or dramatically, early or late, to God.

In this chapter, we are looking at the reasonable grounds, revealed in this terse Gospel, for coming to the intellectual belief that Jesus is both "the man for others" in the late Bishop John Robinson's vivid phrase, and also Jesus, unique, as the "only begotten Son of the Father". But make no mistake about it, we are not as men and women called simply to make an intellectual *appraisal* of who Jesus is. *He* makes a moral appraisal of who *we* are, as sinners before our Holy God and Creator, and if we are still at arm's length from the living Lord, the experiment of discovering who Jesus really is must lead to the adventure of this threefold adventure of a moral, and intellectual, and a volitional response to his direct call "Follow me" (1:17).

If you are seeking a deeper faith in the basic claims of Christ to be the Son of God, then read on, and with Mark's Gospel open, now, before you. He deals with unclean spirits in the Synagogue (1:21–27) at Capernaum. The ruins of the old Synagogue are still there, near the Sea of Galilee. It is easy to imagine Jesus, on that Sabbath day, then moving next door to Simon and Andrew's house, where he healed Simon Peter's mother-in-law so completely, that immediately she was strong enough to serve them in her home (1:29–31).

In the stillness of the Sabbath evening, many came to him for help, and with patience, and long-suffering sympathy, "he healed many" and no doubt "virtue went out of him." We catch a glimpse of this, in that "a great while before day he rose and went out to a lonely place, to pray" (1:35).

Who is this? Son of God, with miraculous power to

heal? – but also very human, in his disciplined but human need to draw his strength in prayer from his heavenly Father, was he not also "Son of Man?"

This chapter of Mark ends with another glimpse of "Godhead and Manhood, who were joined together in one Person" (Article 2) responding to the urgent appeal of a leper, kneeling before Jesus with an earnest request: "If you will, you can make me clean." In his humanity, in love, as he was "moved with compassion" (v. 41) Jesus did what nobody else *would* do – he touched him. Then, in his Deity, in power, he did what nobody else *could* do – he healed him.

During a recent diocesan mission in Uganda, away in the south-west, I visited a former leper colony, reached only by dug-out canoe, and at Kisizi Hospital I saw some of the rehabilitation work for lepers being done there. Two old Ugandan women were having lunch when I called. As a bishop, one (slowly) gets used to laying one's hands on people, young and old, and asking God to bless them. I was surprised within myself, and rather ashamed, that I had to make an effort to smile, lay my hands on their heads, and slowly ask a blessing for them both. Yes, lepers can still feel isolated. Jesus did what no one else *would* do, and *could* do that day. Indeed, we ask, "Who is this?"

Mark 5 is a most vivid account of the power of Jesus over demonic powers assaulting the soul, disease discomforting the body, and "the last enemy", death itself, destroying the earthly life of a young girl. Much of Mark's Gospel stems from Peter's memories. Later (8:29) Jesus asks Peter the direct question: "Who do you say that I am?" to which Peter by then, at Caesarea Philippi, was able to say "You are the Christ." Because "faith comes by hearing and hearing by the Word of God" (Rom. 10:17) or "by the preaching of Christ" study this chapter as if you were looking over Peter's shoulder at his Master. We do not need to conjure up faith emotionally. It is one of God's gifts, experienced when we read the Bible slowly, honestly and in obedience.

The conquest of demonic powers

They came to the other side of the sea, to the country of
the Gerasenes. And when he had come out of the boat,
there met him out of the tombs a man with an unclean
spirit, who lived among the tombs; and no one could
bind him any more, even with a chain; for he had often
been bound with fetters and chains, but the chains he
wrenched apart, and the fetters he broke in pieces; and
no one had strength to subdue him. (Mark 5:1–4.)

Here was brave confrontation between Jesus and a desperately deranged and potentially dangerous man, the
potentially destructive power of a man dominated by
devilish influence, face to face with the brave, strong,
outgoing love of a good man, of a prophet, of the "Son of
the Most High God" (v. 7). The delusions of the demoniac
are swept away and he finds he is confronted by the very
Son of God. Here is ultimate reality, and running from
afar to the feet of Jesus first he shrinks from commitment,
and stands on the brink of decision, and calls "torment me
not" (v. 7) and then, as he leaps across the gap of loneli-
ness and terror to Jesus, he turns and sees the outcast and
ceremonially unclean swine take fright, and perish,
drowned in the sea, and never to be seen again. Plenty of
questions remain around this terrifying story. Yet, which
is more precious, the loss of two thousand swine, or the
reclamation and salvation of one eternal soul, who ever
afterwards "began to proclaim in the Ten Cities how much
Jesus had done for him" (v. 20). Do our responses to the
story reveal our value judgments, rather than our criticism
of the Master? Nothing can be more precious than the
eternal value of one human soul, precious to the Saviour.

The conquest of debilitating disease

And a great crowd followed him and thronged about
him. And there was a woman who had had a flow of
blood for twelve years, and who had suffered much

under many physicians, and had spent all that she had, and was no better but rather grew worse. She had heard the reports about Jesus, and came up behind him in the crowd and touched his garment. For she said, "If I touch even his garments, I shall be made well". And immediately the haemorrhage ceased; and she felt in her body that she was healed of her disease. And Jesus, perceiving in himself that power had gone forth from him, immediately turned about in the crowd, and said, "Who touched me?" And he looked around to see who had done it. But the woman, knowing what had been done to her, came in fear and trembling and fell down before him, and told him the whole truth. And he said to her, "Daughter, your faith has made you well; go in peace, and be healed of your disease."

Mark 5:24–34

There is always light at the end of the tunnel, when we know that our relatives are getting better, but fitful hope would have been dissipated into dark despair, if Jesus had not acted in his loving, miraculous and divine way, in the life of both the former demoniac, and the woman who had had a haemorrhage for twelve years.

The man "had often been bound, but (now) no one had the strength to subdue him" (v. 4). The woman "had suffered much under many physicians, and had spent all that she had and was no better, but rather grew worse" (v. 26).

The harrowing plight of hungry and thirsty refugees, lingering in our memories after the vivid impact of T.V. pictures, reminds us of the sad world we live in. Buddha sits calm, bland, smiling with his soft and gentle hands folded. By contrast, Jesus in the days of his flesh stretched out his hands in love, to touch and soothe, to steady and comfort, to restrain and to heal.

For the demoniac man, he was not afraid and took the initiative to heal him. For the woman, he was not too busy, and stopped to enquire who had taken the initiative, to touch him. "She felt in her body that she was healed of her disease" (v. 29). "He knew in himself that power had gone forth from him" (v. 30). Still it ever is, when in our need and hopelessness we seek to touch "but the hem of His garments" and he in his love and power reaches out to make us whole in the inner recesses of our souls. "Is not this the Christ?"

The conquest of death

Imagination is a God-given faculty, acute in children, and to be retained and developed as we grow older, and it is a special gift to be harnessed to bring people from the confusion of agnosticism, into the sensible field of faith. The Gospel writers, and especially Mark, tell such vivid stories that imagination is kindled, and particularly in the three interlocking stories of chapter 5.

"And when Jesus had crossed again in the boat to the other side, a great crowd gathered about him; and he was beside the sea. Then came one of the rulers of the synagogue, Jairus by name; and seeing him, he fell at his feet, and besought him, saying, 'My little daughter is at the point of death. Come and lay your hands on her, so that she may be made well, and live.' " And he went with him.

Jairus was a believing "ruler of the synagogue", who recognised Jesus' divine power, and may have known of the paralysed man, "ransomed, healed, restored, forgiven" next door to the Capernaum synagogue. His public words are themselves a testimony: "Come and lay your hand on (my little daughter) so that she may be made well and live." His daughter was about to die, and he was so harassed in his soul, yet so believing in his heart, that "he fell at Jesus' feet" and said "Come". Professor A. M. Hunter (formerly Professor of Biblical Criticism, University of Aberdeen), who informed my mind and enriched my soul in his Introduction and Commentary on Mark (S.C.M. Press), enters deeply into this intertwined story of the sick woman, and the twelve-year-old dying girl, writing: "Jairus is not the only person with faith. In the crowd there is a woman whose misery is as old as Jairus' daughter." After Jesus stopped to heal the woman the crowd bustles up, Jeremiah-like, to Jairus, and says with consummate tactlessness and insensitivity, "Don't worry the Rabbi. Your little girl is dead." Hunter quotes D. S. Carus in *The Faith That Rebels*, by reminding us that "Jesus risked his whole reputation in going *on*." "Fear not," Jesus said, ignoring the message, "only go on believing." Few stories seem to bring us closer to the real Jesus of his contemporaries than this one. He was not too busy for the woman who had been ill for twelve years, in fact the year when Jairus and his wife were rejoicing over their baby daughter's birth. He took time to settle the woman with her new-found faith. He would not be rushed. He ignored the gloomy advice of Jairus' friends. He would not let Jairus be discouraged. He openly walked into a house of sudden death, and steadied the family, and dismissed the professional mourners, and cleared the sick room of all but the parents and his own inner circle. All he did was orderly, sensible, calming. Even the first of his three recorded miracles of raising the dead (the little girl, the son of the widow, and Lazarus) was not magical, but methodical. He quietened the room, he shut the door, he held the cold small hand of the twelve-year-old. He spoke quietly to her, with gentleness and reassurance. "Little girl, I say to you, arise," and she sat up. Here is one of the "*Ipsissima verba*", the very words Jesus said: "*Talitha cumi*," in Aramaic, the child's mother tongue. Hunter the Scottish professor writes, "The Authorised Version's 'Damsel, I say unto thee, arise' is far too stiff. In Scots it would be 'My wee lassie, get up.'" Again the injunction to silence. Notice also the humanity of our Lord. How easily he turns from supernatural to natural. "She will need something to eat." Even the child's mother, it has been said, was not so motherly as Jesus.

As you read the other chapters leading up to the questions of Jesus and the profession by Peter at Caesarea Philippi (8:27–30) spend time allowing the Bible to do, by God's Spirit, its contemporary work in every age, of assuring you that this Jesus is the Christ, the Son of God.

What is his purpose?

Not until the Divine Person of Jesus is clearly established, do the Gospel writers speak of the Divine purpose for which he was sent.

"He began to teach them that the Son of Man must suffer many things, and be rejected by the elders and the chief priest, and the scribes, and be *killed*, and *after three days rise again*. And Jesus said this plainly" (8:31, 32). Mark, clearly urged on by Peter, who had at first got it so wrong (8:32, 33), keeps returning to this truth in the second half of his Gospel (see here 8:31–33 and 34–36; also 9:9 and 9:30–32 and more fully 10:32–34 and 14:22–25). Always he spoke of his Resurrection, when he prophesied his death. Critical scholars, finding the plain text a difficulty, offer a rational explanation, that Jesus did *not* make these reiterated statements about "death-and-resurrection" as Archbishop Michael Ramsey puts it, but they were written into the text afterwards. Must we consider that the Apostles lacked integrity, and told untruths, to give spurious comfort to the early Christians, perhaps already facing persecution, as the Synoptic writers produced their Gospels? Conservative scholars observe, however, that if these "death-and-resurrection" passages were later interpretations, they would surely have the appearances, the Ascension, and the promise of the return *also* added.

For myself, I find the reiterated emphases convincing, and in harmony with the most primitive statements about the Cross and Resurrection in 1 Corinthians 15, in the Pentecost Sermons, and in the summary of Acts 17, where in the synagogue at Thessalonica, "for three weeks, Paul *argued* with them from the Scriptures, explaining and proving that it was necessary for the Christ to suffer and to rise from the dead, and saying 'This Jesus, whom I proclaim to you, is the Christ'" (Acts 17:2, 3).

Now watch for the inter-related strands of revealed truth, that are interwoven in Mark chapters 9–16:

1. The sufferings that lay ahead of Christ (9:30, 31; 10:32–34; 10:45; 12:6–8; 14:8; 14:21).

2. The prophecy of his Resurrection, which would follow (9:31; 10:34).
3. The promise of his glory and triumph (9:1–8; 10:30; 11:9, 10 and especially 13:3–37 to the inner group of the original 4 disciples (v. 3) and publicly 14:61, 62).
4. The factual account of his death and Resurrection in chapters 14–16, with the sacrificial overtones of the Passover sacrifice (14:1, 2; 14:12) in the context of the Lord's Supper, or Holy Communion (14:17–28), finishing with the often reiterated words (v. 28) "But after I am raised up, I will go before you to Galilee."

Apart from the long apocalyptic discourse (Mark 13:3–37), Mark's taut, dramatic, factual narrative moves unfalteringly through the last days of Christ on earth, and the central figure of Jesus never seems to leave the centre of the stage. The discourse suggests the layered teaching of Jesus on the three critical levels of Cross and Resurrection, of immediate coming trial, disaster and tribulation, and of final triumph and return, centring in the climax of the promise:

"And then they will see the Son of Man coming in clouds with great power and glory" (13:26) leading to the majestic prophecy of Christianity established as a world religion: "Then he will send out the angels and gather the elect from the four winds from the ends of the earth to the end of time" (v. 27).

Although critics cast doubt on the authenticity of parts of Mark 13 it must be remembered that Mark records that at the time these prophetic and apocalyptic words were uttered, they were only shared (13:3) "privately to Peter" (Mark's source) "and James and John and Andrew", who were not only the core quartet of the apostolic band but, apart from Andrew, also the inner circle chosen by Jesus to be with him on the Mount of Transfiguration (9:2–10) when he was revealed as Messiah and Son of God, within the Shekinah Glory of God's Presence (9:7) and again promised to come in his glory, at the end of time (13:26).

As Mary was probably Luke the physician's source for the special revelation of the Lord's humanity and his miraculous conception, so Peter would have been Mark's source for the special revelation of Jesus as Messiah and coming King. Mark 14:51 has the strange interpolation, which may well refer to young Mark himself:

"And a young man followed him, with nothing but a linen cloth about his body; and they seized him, but he left the linen cloth and ran away naked." This fast-moving and vivid Gospel ends as breathlessly as it began. Not only did the young man run fast (14:51) but the women at the open and empty tomb, still unable to believe the sheer objective miracle told by the "young man in a white robe" (16:5) that "He is not here, he is risen" (v. 6), "went out and fled from the tomb, trembling and astonished". In their fear and amazement did they think that the angelic messenger was in fact the young man in the linen cloth of 14:51?

The sheer rough edges of the narrative, with the disputed endings of Mark's Gospel (see the various MSS in the RSV edition of the New Testament), provide us with a challenge. Are we reading a hastily cobbled together "apologia" to cheer frightened disciples in the early Church? Is this a pious fabrication? Was Jesus not raised from the grave on the third day in a bodily form, recognisable from the past, but transformed in the present?

Here again is the tragic divide in religious thinking today.

Or are the very loose ends of the Easter narratives, and the statement that the early disciples were so slow to believe this supreme Easter miracle of Resurrection, that only the sheer stubborn miraculous event can account for their move forward from doubt to faith, from sorrow to happiness, from trembling fear to joyous hope? Surely what happened to raise Jesus from the dead in his resurrected body on the third day was already so much part of their immediate experience of the Risen Lord, that a week later, with Thomas now with them in the Upper Room of the first Eucharist, they can say "We have *seen* the Lord."

Here is the vital difference in a scholarly approach to

the Bible. Some try to find areas of possible disagreement in the sacred text. Other scholars seek positively for the directions in which the harmonising of the texts reveal deeper and broader truth.

Dr. John Stott in his *Times* article, "Reflections on the Resurrection", speaks of the Resurrection of Jesus as a "divine act of vindication. Moreover, since the verdict had been public, its reversal needed to be public too." John Stott continues:

Paul is clear about what happened on that third day. His statement of the gospel (which he claimed was taught and believed throughout the church) was that Christ died for our sins, that he was buried, that he was raised on the third day, and that he was seen by witnesses. The focus was on the death and Resurrection of Jesus, while the burial attested the reality of the death and the appearances the reality of the Resurrection. How, then, can it be said that Paul did not believe in the empty tomb? The four verbs ("died", "was buried", "was raised" and "appeared") all have Christ as their subject, and must logically all refer to his body.

I cannot see that we have liberty to declare the death and burial to have been physical, while the Resurrection and appearances were not. True, when the dead and buried body of Jesus was raised, it was changed in the process (it is incredible that Bultmann dismissed the Resurrection as if it were "the resuscitation of a corpse").

But when Paul wrote that Christ "died, was buried, was raised and appeared", we may be sure that he did not mean that he was raised *while still remaining buried*. No, what was buried was raised. So the tomb must have been empty.

Of course scholars discuss the texts surrounding this event, and some apparent inconsistencies spur Biblical scholars to a deeper study of the Biblical evidence. In earlier days, Morison in *Who Moved the Stone?* (Faber and Faber) came to faith by studying the differences, as they at first seem, in the four Gospels. In this decade, John Wenham, a senior conservative scholar, approached the story of the Resurrection as Dorothy Sayers might have done. His substantial work *Easter Enigma* (Paternoster Press) is a fine work of positive harmonising and will deepen faith at intellectual level, revealing as it does an almost contemporary atmosphere, concerning the probable locations of the various members of the apostolic band in the three or four houses where they would have rested on the Sabbath after Good Friday. As an example of the negative approach, because Luke and John speak of two angels at the tomb while Mark tells only of "the young man in white" (see above), critics doubt the authority of the narratives concerned. A. M. Hunter, who is not an avowed conservative, yet quotes Lessing approvingly: "Cold discrepancy-mongers, do you not see then that evangelists do not count the angels? There were not only two angels, there were millions of them!"

Wenham in his *Easter Enigma* rightly calls for a redress of the balance from a negative criticism that casts aspersions on the integrity of the human Gospel writers, and on the trustworthiness of the Easter witnesses, to a more positive recognition of the providential nature of the primitive manuscripts, with the Rylands Fragment (AD 120–150) as an example. Of major importance are the critics' subconscious pre-suppositions. Are these documents human writings, written with a slanted perspective to defend the early Church's position? Or as Peter put it bluntly, "No prophecy ever came by the impulse of man, but moved by the Holy Spirit, holy men spoke from God" (2 Peter 1:21) in support of Paul's affirmation: "All Scripture is inspired by God and (is) profitable for teaching, for reproof, for correction and for training in righteousness" (2 Timothy 3:16).

In our honest search for a faith in Christ, which is not only morally challenging, but intellectually satisfying, and so spiritually rewarding, we must look at the Bible itself, so we now look at what is still by far the world's "bestseller".

Parallel with this search, however, can go the sheer self-authenticating experience of slowly, honestly and obediently reading, for instance, Mark's Gospel which has been in our minds in this chapter. As we read of this solitary figure, Jesus, we can be led to ask: is he mad? He made stupendous claims at least in secret to his disciples claiming he would "rise from the dead" and "come again in the clouds" (Mark 9:7–10; 13:24–27). Jesus, is he bad? He invited people to trust him to forgive their sins, which is the prerogative of God alone (2:10), and apparently did healing miracles over paralysis (2:9) and even over death itself (Mark 5:39–43) to prove his power, as well as to meet need with compassion.

If not mad, or bad, is he not indeed God incarnate? For many, good news by Mark becomes knowledge that leads to faith, despite the persistent intellectual strait-jacket that "miracles do not happen" as the elder Huxley once put it. A hundred years ago Matthew Arnold, with his famous gospel of "Sweet Reasonableness", spent a great deal of time trying to evolve a non-miraculous Christianity, and there are traces of this century-old debility in the present Archbishop of York's reported statement in *The Times* that he approaches miracles "with an open mind". There is something essentially mysterious about this library of sixty-six books we call "the Bible", and I for my part believe that sheer inescapable "miracle" is inseparable from it, and that a broad and satisfying experience of God in Christ cannot be found, without recognising that our Lord's life from birth to death and from Resurrection to Ascension, is a procession of God-ordained and God-executed miracles.

How can we be sure that the Bible is the Word of God? This is the theme of our next chapter.

9

HOW CAN I TRUST THE BIBLE?

I remember a young man in Oxford, who had tried everything: modern music, advanced politics, and unusual clothes. He came to me one day and told me that he now wanted to try religion, and so had begun to read the Bible, beginning at Genesis, but he wondered if this straightforward chronological way to read it was best.

It has been said: "It was the primary function of the Scriptures to bear witness to Christ. Christ was the key that unlocked the Scriptures, and the Hebrew Scriptures were a Christian and not only a Jewish book. Henceforward the Scriptures must be read in the light of Jesus' Resurrection; the Spirit of the Risen Christ would interpret to the Christian reader the things in all the Scriptures concerning himself."

I suggested to the young man in Oxford that he should begin reading John's Gospel, because here God came close to us through the Lord Jesus Christ. He would find the deepest meaning of the Bible plainly put, "Christ in all the Scriptures" (Luke 24:26, 27), as the revelation of God to show us what God is really like, and as our Sin-bearer and Saviour to bring us to God, and as our living Lord and Friend, when we commit ourselves to him in adventurous faith.

John 1:14: "The Word became flesh and dwelt among us, full of grace and truth; we have beheld his glory, glory as of the only Son from the Father."

John 1:29: "Behold the Lamb of God, who takes away the sin of the world!"

John 20:30, 31: "And Jesus did many other signs in the presence of his disciples, which are not written in this book; but these are written that you may believe that Jesus is the Christ, the Son of God, and that believing you may have life in his name."

John's Gospel, with perhaps the vivid and almost cinematic Gospel of Mark, together make both the story of Jesus, and the purposes behind the narrative, live to us, so that we find the Holy Spirit doing his special work of revealing Jesus Christ to us as Incarnate God, dying Sin-bearer, and living Lord. And so the Holy Spirit leads us to repentance, faith in Christ, and obedience to his will, which in turn sets our feet upon the road of true Christian discipleship, in the fellowship of the family of God, Christ's Church.

As he read the Bible in this way, this young man was led to put his whole trust and confidence in Christ, and later I had the privilege of preparing him for Baptism and Confirmation and later he was ordained.

He approached the question of the inspiration and authority of Scripture from two points of view. First, he tried to discover the purpose for which the Scriptures were written, namely to reveal Jesus Christ to every generation. Secondly, he saw that writers like John claimed to be writing for this purpose (John 20:30, 31, with its frankly propagandist tone), and he boldly experimented by taking them at their word, and testing their claims by steadily and systematically reading the Bible itself.

Let us now look more fully at the purposes for which the Scriptures were written, and then at the methods which God used for their production.

The purposes for which Scripture was written

The Bible contains a wealth of historical, scientific, ethical, philosophical, political and poetic material, but the Book has been preserved for us, by God's providence, for an essentially practical purpose, so that in every age men may find in Scripture the offer of God's salvation through

Christ, and through Scripture may learn how to live in daily fellowship with God, that men might worship their Creator and serve humanity in this life, and be received into his immediate Presence for all eternity, after death.

A careful study of such a key passage as 2 Timothy 3:14–17 makes this plain, and explains and amplifies other similar passages in the Bible.

a) *The Bible makes us wise about salvation*

"From childhood you have been acquainted with the sacred writings which are able to instruct you for salvation through faith in Christ Jesus" (2 Tim 3:15).

We noticed that "it was the primary function of the Scriptures to bear witness to Christ". When on the first Easter Day two disciples were returning home to Emmaus, crestfallen and confused, Jesus met them, and explained that if they studied the Old Testament they would see that Jesus of Nazareth fulfilled the prophecies about the Christ or the Anointed One, and that his death was not just a tragic and inexplicable accident, but was the fulfilment of the prophecies that Christ should bear our sins in his death upon the Cross, and then rise to be our living and triumphant Saviour (Luke 24:45–47). This salvation becomes a present experience when men trust in the name of Christ, and so find forgiveness of sins, peace with God, and new life by the indwelling of the Holy Spirit.

This salvation is now offered to all men for "God desires *all* men to be saved" (1 Timothy 2:3, 4) but it is revealed by the Holy Spirit in the Scriptures with such simplicity and certainty that a child can understand (2 Timothy 3:15) and this wisdom is the essential knowledge that all men need, and that the Scriptures provide.

The first purpose leads naturally to the second:

b) *The Bible shows us the way of sanctification*

"All Scripture is inspired by God and profitable for

teaching, for reproof, for correction, and for training in righteousness" (2 Timothy 3:16).

The forgiveness of our former sins, and the setting right of our past rebellion against God, would be unprofitable indeed if we did not discover the secrets of victory in temptation, and the road to sanctification or holiness of life.

The Bible shows us Christ, by his Cross, providing us with all the pardon we need to be right with God; then we discover Christ in us, by his Spirit, providing us with all the power we need to live a holy life (Romans 8:9–11; Galatians 5:16, 17).

Jesus said "Abide in me, and I in you . . . You are already made clean by the word which I have spoken to you" (John 15:4, 3).

The Bible explains God's provision for holy living, in doctrinal terms. A life-long study of it will lead us to face the detailed challenge of daily surrender to his will; the call to the complete consecration of our ambitions to the revelation of his purpose for us; and the consequent infilling of our increasingly obedient hearts by his holy and powerful Spirit. There are no short cuts to spiritual maturity, so do not grasp at exotic manifestations of spiritual excitement, but rather grow in grace, and in the knowledge of the Lord Jesus, by following the example of the first Christians in Berea, who examined the Scriptures daily "to see if these things were so" (Acts 17:11).

Not only do the Scriptures show us how the Holy Spirit sanctifies believing Christians, but the very study of the Bible does its own work of keeping our consciences sensitive, our minds pure, and the face of the Lord Jesus personally turned towards us. In the written Word we see Jesus the living Word.

> Turn your eyes upon Jesus,
> Look full in his wonderful face,
> And the things of earth will grow strangely
>   dim,
> In the light of his glory and grace.

c) *The Bible equips us for Christ's service*

If as a child we become wise unto salvation (2 Timothy 3:15) and as a young person learn the secret of sanctification, or holiness of life (2 Timothy 3:16), we never grow beyond the study of the Bible, when as a full-grown man or woman we seek to learn how to serve Christ all our days (2 Timothy 3:17).

I was particularly reminded of this in my past work as Principal of a theological college, where we were preparing men for ordination, because the Ordinal in the Book of Common Prayer, and the A.S.B. of 1980 lay such stress upon a deep and ever-growing knowledge of the Bible.

It is not enough to suggest that the formularies of the ordinal are outdated just because they are historical, for the prime authority of the Bible in the Church of England is basic to its continuance as both Catholic and Reformed. If he wants to believe *less* an intending ordinand can apply for training as a Unitarian minister. If he wants to believe *more* than the Bible he can offer for training for the Roman Catholic priesthood. To Scripture, the Roman Catholic Church adds to matters of faith extra matters, like the bodily assumption of Mary into Heaven, and the infallibility of the Pope, which were both added to the doctrines that a Roman Catholic ordinand must believe.

The Church of England, with its gentle discipline, invites conscientious commitment to Christian doctrine found in Scripture: no more, no less, and no ordinand is forced into statements he doesn't believe, for he has three years or so to come to his clear conclusions.

What is true for the clergy is also true for any man or woman who desires to serve Christ fully and fruitfully.

Only so will our service for Christ have lasting results in the lives of others.

These, then, are the three basic purposes for which the Scriptures are given. When these purposes are becoming increasingly fulfilled in our own lives, we come to believe in the authority and inspiration of the Bible, first from our own experience of Christ, then from our growth in the Christian life with our fellow-Christians in the fellowship of Christ's Church, and finally from whatever limited results we have seen in our Christian service. We believe the Bible is the Word of God "because it works".

The pragmatic view will become increasingly real to the Christian, but it needs to be supported by the plain propositions on inspiration mentioned next. However, men cannot be argued into believing that the Bible is the Word of God.

As we live in a climate of opinion which is often narrow-minded, unthinking and even proud about denigrating the authority of the Bible, these reasons may be a help. The narrow-minded view I mention supposes that the Bible is *only* written by men; that it is no different from any other "inspiring" book; that it must be out of date because it is ancient; and that man has so "come of age" intellectually, that he has grown beyond the Scriptures. In fact, man, without the revelation of God in Christ through the Scriptures, has become a cross between an atomic giant and an ethical pigmy, and would be hopeless indeed, if God in his mercy had not broken into this helpless condition by his revelation of himself in the Scriptures, and in his Son.

However, many young people are affected by the view that the Bible is "just another book", held by older people who have never bothered to discover why the traditional view of the Divine authority of Holy Scripture is of such importance for an assured, confident and victorious Christian life. For instance, Article 6 of the Thirty-nine Articles says, "Holy Scripture containeth all things necessary to salvation." Canon 5 (revised since the last World War) states the present position in the Church of England when it now says, "The doctrine of the Church of England is grounded in the Holy Scriptures, and in such teachings of the ancient Fathers and Councils of the Church as are agreeable to the said Scriptures, and in particular to be found in the Thirty-nine Articles of Religion, the Book of Common Prayer, and the Ordinal."

Every young man at his ordination is asked, "Do you accept the Holy Scriptures as revealing all things necessary for eternal salvation through faith in Jesus Christ?"

How Was the Bible Written?
What should we think, therefore, of the Bible, and why should we consider it to be the unique Word of God, and not only a collection of the words of men?

Clearing Away the Misconceptions
The traditional or conservative view of Scripture does not accept a "dictation" view, as though to say that God used the human authors as mechanical teleprinters. Bishop Cockin, thinking this was the conservative view, wrote, "God does not destroy the personality of the man whom he inspires by using him as a dictaphone." Of course not! Anyone reading Paul's fiery and even disjointed letters in a modern translation would not call Paul stifled, or "destroyed", and yet he himself wrote, "All Scripture is inspired by God" (2 Timothy 3:16), and Peter recognised that Scripture consisted of Paul's writings just as much as of the prophets (2 Pet. 3:15, 16).

In the same way, the processes of detailed study of sources of material, described by Luke himself (Luke 1:1) of "form" criticism, and of the painstaking discovery of older manuscripts, together with archaeological finds in the Near East, need not affect the traditional view of the unique authority of Scripture, as is seen in the scholarly studies on Biblical subjects in, for instance, the New Bible Commentary and the New Bible Dictionary, both published by Inter-Varsity Press.

The Bible is not like the Koran, which Muslims think fell from Heaven already written, but its very complexities provide an incentive for the thoughtful Christian to explore its depths, as the astronomer explores God's universe. Whereas the scientist can only experiment and record what he sees, leaving the rest to intelligent guesswork, the Christian soon discovers that the Holy Spirit, whom the Scripture maintains is the Divine Author, is now also the Revealer of Truth to those who are themselves regenerated by the same Spirit. In fact, the Scripture is used to arouse faith in the Lord Jesus (John 16:13–15 and Romans 10:17), and when faith is kindled the Bible speaks "from faith to faith". The Reverend Alec Motyer has said, "God pledged his Spirit to explain his Word to us," commenting on 1 Cor. 2:9–14, which is a key passage in this context.

The Balance of Authorship

Peter wrote: "Men moved by the Holy Spirit spoke from God" (2 Peter 1:21). Paul also said: "We impart this in words not taught by human wisdom but taught by the Spirit, interpreting spiritual truths to those who possess the Spirit" (1 Cor. 2:13).

The Bible is a library of sixty-six books by many authors, in a number of major languages, mainly Hebrew and Greek, but with traces of Chaldean and Aramaic. The authors span hundreds of years, and are of many backgrounds, temperaments, cultures and abilities.

The quiet, sensitive Ezra plucks out the hairs of his beard when he confesses the sins of the people (Ezra 9:3). The bluff, extrovert Nehemiah, Ezra's near contemporary, pulls the hair from other people's beards! (Nehemiah 13:25).

Peter's practical simplicity is in marked contrast to Paul's intellectual convolutions of phrase. No wonder – to use an idea from the English school system – Peter (an Ordinary or "O" Level man) finds Paul (an Advanced or "A" Level man) hard to understand! (See 2 Peter 3:16) The different approach of the Synoptic Gospel writers gives a "3-D" stereoscopic and stereophonic effect, in depth, to the Gospels, revealed to our inward eyes and ears. The Revd. John Stott writes, "The literary style of the writers is different, and their theological emphasis is different and individual. Further, we believe these differences within the unity of the Bible are due to the Holy Spirit's deliberate purpose. It is not an accident, for instance, that Amos was the prophet of God's justice, Hosea of his love, Isaiah of his sovereignty and unity, and Jeremiah of his individualism. Nor is it an accident in the New Testament that Paul was the apostle of grace and faith, John of love, Peter of hope, and James of works."

There is, therefore, a rich diversity in the jewel-box of Holy Scripture. At the same time, there is a remarkable unity which runs through the Book, as we recognise one God, one scheme of salvation, one emphasis on man's sin, one family of his Church, one Christ who has come and will come again, and one Heaven to which all believers in Christ will one day come. The substance of the Old Testament revelation may have been partial, but it was truly preparatory for the consummation of the New Testament in Christ; the whole of truth is not revealed in the Old Testament, but it is selective truth which is congruous to the full truth shown forth in Christ, not error to be countermanded in the New.

Both the Israelites in the Old Testament, and the Christians in the New, had their Book (Old Testament and New Testament), their Sacrifice (Passover and Calvary), their initiatory sacrament (Circumcision and Baptism), their Meeting Places with God (Tabernacle, Temple or Church) and a personal challenge to respond to God's grace (faith in both cases: Genesis 15:6 and Ephesians 2:8). The congruity of truth in the Old Testament and New Testament, and the unity which runs through the Book can have but one rational explanation. The human authors were not groping blindly to discover hidden truths. The Divine Author, God himself by his Holy Spirit, was revealing his mind and purposes, as they were able to receive the unfolding truth, until he completed this revelation in the person and work of his Son, and explained this revelation through the chosen Apostles of Christ's day. The amount of revelation might differ: there will be, in our present day, more revealed truth in John 15 than in an Old Testament genealogy. The principle of inspiration does not alter. It is still God speaking. The word "inspiration" means "God-breathed", so that we may think of God not merely giving the writers their ideas, but breathing out his thoughts through their sanctified personalities.

The Divine Authority for Divine Authorship

Is this a human theory of inspiration, even though it is summarised by Peter, taught by Paul and explained by the writer to the Hebrews? Surely not. Look at these verses again.

"No prophecy ever came by the impulse of man, but men moved by the Holy Spirit spoke from God" (2 Peter 1:21).

"All Scripture is inspired by God" (2 Timothy 3:16).

"In many and various ways God spoke of old to our fathers by the prophets; but in these last days he has spoken to us by a Son, whom he appointed the heir of all things, through whom also he created the world" (Hebrews 1:1, 2).

Surely if God has created us, and loves us, he would want us to find him with certainty and enjoyment? We have seen that the purpose of Scripture is man's salvation. There may be intellectual difficulties about inspiration, but logically it is simple. If God is a God of love, personally concerned with his created beings, he wants us to find him for ourselves.

There are two main reasons why we should trust the Bible: first the Bible's own explicit and implicit claims, and secondly Christ's own estimate of the authority of Scripture, although there are other factors of great importance in support of this belief. At the same time, the archaeological, literary, and theological reasons for belief in the authority of Scripture are of great relevance.

I have myself sat on the side of Jacob's Well at Sychar, where Jesus sat (John 4:6). I have knelt in the garden of Gethsemane where Jesus prayed (Mark 14:32) and I have stood on the Lithostrotos or "the Pavement" in the Antonia Fortress in Jerusalem where he was tried, mocked, and scourged and condemned (Matt. 27:27). The wealth of archaeological discovery in recent years underlines so much of Scripture's historicity. A book like Sir Charles Marston's *The Bible is True* (Eyre and Spottiswoode), though written as far back as 1934, is still thrilling reading. "When was the New Testament written? At the turn of this century, the span extended from about AD 50 to about AD 150 – by the middle of the century, with the isolated exception of one book, it was halved, from about AD 50 to AD 100.

"I am personally of the opinion that it should be halved *again*, from about AD 47 to just before AD 70." Although he warns the reader that other N.T. scholars would not agree with him, this witness to the early writing of the New Testament is a powerful argument towards the accuracy of our knowledge of the New Testament (page 63).

In his later book *Can We Trust the New Testament?* (Mowbray), Bishop John Robinson (no self-confessed conservative) returned from his *Honest to God* days to a positive approach to the Bible which is very refreshing.

The constant growth of literary evidence, such as the discoveries of the Rylands Fragment, the Chester Beatty papyri, and other older Biblical manuscripts, gives us even more accurate ideas of the original documents. The Rylands Fragment, in the John Rylands Library, Manchester, is dated not later than AD 150 and is a Greek excerpt from John 18:31–33, 37, 38.

As I write this, I hold in my other hand a piece of pottery that I picked up at Q'mran, where the Essenes had their community, near the shores of the deep blue of the Dead Sea, looking over to the rugged and beautiful mountains of Moab, beyond Jordan. Here many first-century documents have recently been found that throw light on Scripture. They are generally called the Dead Sea Scrolls, and they must have been written before AD 68, for the Essenes hid their manuscripts on receiving the warning that the Romans were coming that way to sack Jerusalem under Vespasian in AD 70.

In addition to archaeological and literary finds, the theological reasons for belief in the inspiration of

Scripture are set out in many books today, ranging from brief introductory studies to deeper and fuller works covering a much wider field than this chapter.

The Claims of the Bible itself

We have already seen that in 2 Timothy 3:16 and in 2 Peter 1:21, the Biblical authors make explicit claims to Divine authority and authorship, but the implicit and seemingly "passing" references to the Bible being God's Word written, are equally striking.

Many authors constantly write "Thus says the Lord" and claim that God is himself speaking directly through his servant to his people. Study the promise to Moses in Deuteronomy 18:15–20; to David in 2 Samuel 23:2, "The Spirit of the Lord speaks by me, his word is upon my tongue"; to Isaiah in Isaiah 9:8, "The Lord has sent a word against Jacob, and it will light upon Israel"; to Jeremiah in Jeremiah 1:9 and 2:1, "Behold I have put my words in your mouth" and similarly to Ezekiel (Ezek. 1:1).

The element of direct prophecy and its historical fulfilment in Christ, which we ourselves can see in the New Testament story, strengthens our faith in the God-breathed quality of Scripture. The principle is revealed in Deuteronomy 18:15–20, and I suggest that the following fascinating Bible Study in answered prophecy concerning Christ's birth will strengthen the faith of any eager Bible student, for "Faith cometh by hearing, and hearing by the word of God" (Romans 10:17 AV). See Micah 5:2 and Matthew 2:1–6; Isaiah 7:14 and Luke 1:30–35; Isaiah 9:6 and Luke 1:32; Isaiah 53:3–12 and Acts 8:32–5.

The understanding of the New Testament writers was that prophecy was authorised by God, and that the fulfilment of Christ's coming, or coming again, was to be expected. Matthew constantly speaks of this fulfilment, because he particularly had Jews in mind when he was writing (Matthew 1:22; 2:15; 2:17; 2:23; 4:14; 8:17, etc).

The authoritative note in the Apostles' preaching after

Pentecost stemmed from their assurance, not only that Christ had conquered, as shown forth at Easter, but that the Word of God through his prophets said that Christ would be victorious. Peter said, "God foretold by the mouth of all the prophets . . ." (Acts 3:18).

Philip had no hesitation in preaching Jesus to the Ethiopian from Isaiah 53, for Christ himself had said that this very chapter referred to him (Luke 22:37). The Old Testament, though limited in its content, and progressive in its revelation, was not simply the imaginings of fallible men, but the revelation of a loving God through his chosen human instruments, so, as the Church of England teaches:

"The Old Testament is not contrary to the New: for both in the Old and New Testament everlasting life is offered to Mankind by Christ, who is the only Mediator between God and Man, being both God and Man. Wherefore they are not to be heard, which feign that the old Fathers did look only for transitory promises." (Article 7 of the Thirty-nine Articles)

The Teaching of Christ about the Old Testament

These principles of Biblical authority are not only enunciated by the prophets, or embedded in the text of Scripture itself, but taught by the authority of the Lord Jesus himself.

He called the Jewish Scriptures, "the Word of God" (Mark 7:13); he said that the Scriptures could not be broken (John 10:35) and that they spoke about him (John 5:39 and Matthew 26:54). Jesus had prophesied that "on the third day" he would rise from the dead and on the afternoon of Easter Day itself, with Cross and Resurrection now behind him, he immediately began to explain the paradox of the Old Testament. It was not only an historical book, telling of God's guiding hand upon his chosen people, the Jewish family, but like the wheatgerm in the corn of wheat which falls into the ground and dies, it is a prophetic book, that relates the Messiah to the new people of God, the Church of Christ in the new age, and brings forth the message of the "Spirit of Life in Christ Jesus" (Romans 8:2).

Luke 24 repays unhurried reading. Two of his disciples, sad, bemused, still on the dark side of the Cross and the grave of Jesus in their thinking, with heads bowed and "looking sad" had "come to a standstill" actually and figuratively (v. 17). They did not recognise Jesus the travelling companion who fell into step beside them on their seven-mile walk back to their home at Emmaus, across the fields from Jerusalem. Gently he drew out from them the events of the first Holy Week (vv. 18–24). Luke the careful historian gives us here the fullest and most sensitive account of the mental and psychological state in which these two disciples, typical of others, found themselves on that first Easter Day. Even here, that haunting phrase "now the third day" (v. 21) is embedded in their still unbelieving sub-conscious mind. So the Master had often promised. So the angels had that morning said ". . . and on the third day, must rise" (v. 7). So Paul received the early "Kerygma" (the kernel of the Gospel message), as he set it out in 1 Corinthians 15:4. So the early Church built this clear time mark into its Creeds, and "*this* is our faith" as I have dared to call this book.

Now, because of the supreme importance of understanding the miraculous fact and the theological importance of both Christ's real dying and real rising Jesus painstakingly begins "to open to them the Scriptures", which at that time were the Old Testament alone. "O foolish men, and slow of heart to believe all that the prophets have spoken! Was it not necessary that *the Christ* should suffer these things and enter into his glory? And beginning with Moses and all the prophets he interpreted to them in all the Scriptures the things concerning himself" (Luke 24:25–27).

Once again it was suffering and glory; Cross and Resurrection; apparent defeat but open victory.

Although there is no apparent risen appearance of Jesus to his enemies or to unbelievers, there is now a threefold chord offered as a lifeline to every honest seeker after God: the open tomb, empty for all to see; the open

Scriptures, explained for all to understand; the opened lips of the assured disciples (24:22–24) proclaiming to all who would hear that Christ was raised from the dead "on the third day" (v. 6). This threefold chord can still be ours today, if we still have honest doubts, but doubts only remain honest if they are not lazy. There is nothing meritorious in intellectual doubts about the validity of Christ's Resurrection, if we have not reached for this threefold chord, of the historicity of Jesus, of the living witness today of his disciples, and of the painstaking and prayerful study not only of New, but Old Testament.

When my wife and I returned from a visit to the Church of Papua New Guinea, and my son and I returned from the Church in Uganda, both churches having known martyrdom in the hundred years of their respective histories, it gave all of us in our family a deep respect for the living faith of young Christians in these two beautiful countries.

A young Christian Ugandan student, saying goodbye to our son John, writes ". . . If we don't meet again on earth, let's fight the good fight, and make sure we meet in Heaven," and sends Revelation 21:1–8 as a greeting ". . . God himself shall be with them. He will wipe away every tear from their eyes, and death shall be no more, neither shall there be mourning, nor crying nor pain any more, for the former things are passed away. And he who sat upon the throne said 'Behold, I make all things new'."

This was the mature and joyful faith, mirrored in that young Ugandan's greeting, that steadily the Risen Lord was seeking for his confused and sad disciples, on that first Easter Day, twenty centuries earlier, when he said to them as he walked with them: "Was it not *necessary* that the Christ (the Messiah, the Son of God) should suffer these things (which you tell me happened to Jesus your master), and enter into his glory? And beginning with Moses and all the prophets (and the Psalms) he interpreted to them in all the Scriptures the things concerning himself" (Luke 24:26, 27).

Perhaps I am writing for someone for whom sorrow or

bereavement, bitter failure or discouragement, or illness or strain, seems to make faith too difficult an adventure? Jesus truly understands your situation. He did not only shed his precious blood for the forgiveness of your sins and mine upon the Cross. Also, in the secret agony in the Garden of Gethsemane, the battle of the will, and the extreme tension of the situation, were so fierce that Luke the physician actually records the pathological symptom of extreme tension: "Being in an agony Jesus prayed more earnestly; and his sweat became like great drops of blood falling down upon the ground" (Luke 22:44).

Luke may be your "special book" at this time, so take seriously Christ's call to study the Bible for yourself, and notice how not only the New Testament centres in Jesus Christ, but the Old Testament too.

I have seen many more people turn *to* faith in Christ in adversity than *turn away* from him, so take heart, if you are going through a dark valley. Recently, I met in Canada a fine young Church Army captain with inoperable cancer. As we talked of Christ and of suffering, he smiled and said to me, "Bishop, this is no time for doubting."

Jesus in his loving kindness means us so to study the Bible, as the revealed truth about God, that we may come to assurance of salvation through faith in Christ *now*, in the quiet days, so that we can face the storm, when it comes, unafraid. This has been my experience in times of extreme danger and personal bereavement and I believe the fulness of the Christian faith provides just such a threefold lifeline.

We return now to an even more startling statement of Christ about the Bible. Once, where there is a reference to the *text* of Holy Scripture, Jesus says that God himself said the very words found in the narrative (Matt. 22:43). In this way, he called the Scriptures oracular (see Matt. 19:4, 5 compared with Genesis 2:24). He explained that when David, the human author, was speaking, the Holy Spirit of God was inspiring him. David's writings in Scripture were "God-breathed", as explained above in 2 Timothy 3:16.

In the same way, as the late Alan Richardson, formerly Dean of York, points out in his *Theological Word Book of the Bible* (S.C.M. Press), the New Testament authors speak of the Old Testament writers in similar terms: "New Testament writers quote Scripture (usually the Greek Bible, the Septuagint) as the direct utterance of God himself," and he quotes Ephesians 4:8, Hebrews 3:7 (quoting Psalm 95) and Luke 1:70. In Peter's First Epistle, he emphasises his belief in the Holy Spirit's authorship of the Old Testament Scriptures, and in the Second Epistle links Paul's present writings with the Old Testament prophets under the general heading of "the Scriptures".

"The prophets who prophesied of the grace that was to be yours searched and inquired about this salvation; they inquired what person or time was indicated by the Spirit of Christ within them when predicting the sufferings of Christ and the subsequent glory" (1 Peter 1:10–11).

"And count the forbearance of our Lord as salvation. So also our beloved brother Paul wrote to you according to the wisdom given him, speaking of this as he does in all his letters. There are some things in them hard to understand, which the ignorant and unstable twist to their own destruction, *as they do the other scriptures*" (2 Peter 3:15–16).

The promises of Christ for the New Testament

This remarkable unity of interpretation concerning the inspiration of Scripture refers mainly, except for the reference here set out from 2 Peter, to the Old Testament. So what of the New Testament? We would expect that if the Old Testament was "inspired by God" (2 Timothy 3:16) the New Testament, with its more developed truth, seen in the life and work of Christ, would be equally inspired. In fact, before his death, in the unhurried talk with his disciples in the Upper Room, the Lord Jesus makes explicit reference to the work of the Holy Spirit in the Divine Authorship and Supreme Authority of the New Testament, in a manner entirely congruous to the Spirit's work in the Old Testament.

The New Testament would contain historic facts about Christ's words and works; this teaching would be the basis of the early Church's preaching; and there would also be an element of prophecy concerning Christ's return and the Final Judgment.

In explicit promises, Jesus speaks of the stamp of God's authority, which would rest upon the Apostles and the apostolic men, commissioned for this vital task.

"The Counsellor, the Holy Spirit, whom the Father will send in my name, he will teach you all things, and bring to your remembrance all that I have said to you" (John 14:26).

"When the Spirit of truth comes, he will guide you into all the truth, for he will not speak on his own authority, but whatever he hears he will speak; and he will declare to you the things that are to come. He will glorify me, for he will take what is mine and declare it to you" (John 16:13, 14).

When the New Testament was received, with the Old, into the Canon (or rule) of Holy Scripture, the Church did not give the Bible its authority. The Church, led by the Holy Spirit, simply recognised the unique and intrinsic authority within the Scriptures, given to us, so that in many translations, and in every age, men might know enough to see Christ in the Scriptures, and trust him as Saviour and Lord.

As clergy, and particularly as a bishop, we as ministers of the Word as well as ministers of the Sacraments, are called to follow the apostolic pattern, of plain and balanced exposition of Scripture in its plain grammatical sense. Christ took the Old Testament as the authoritative Word of God, and explained it reverently and slowly, and we can do no less.

In Acts 2:29–36 Peter speaks here of David's death and burial in the tomb, which is "with us to this day". By triumphant contrast he speaks of David as a prophet, who foresaw and spoke "of the resurrection of Christ, that he was not abandoned to Hades, nor did his flesh see corruption". Peter then confidently proclaims "This Jesus, God raised up, and of that we all are witnesses" (v. 32). Again supporting his statement by another prophecy of David (Acts 2:34–35) he reaches his triumphant conclusion, "Let all the house of Israel therefore know assuredly that God has made him both Lord and Christ; this Jesus whom you crucified" (2:36).

I happen to be writing this chapter on Whit Monday, when yesterday in Wymondham Abbey, in Norfolk, at a Baptism, Confirmation and First Communion, I had been preaching these same great truths of the whole Catholic Church world-wide, based four-square on Holy Scripture.

Peter boldly asserts: "David foresaw and spoke of the resurrection of Christ, that he was *not* abandoned to Hades (the place of departed spirits), nor did his flesh see corruption" (2:31). Peter then reiterates that God did the miracle of raising him, and he and the Apostles had the privilege of witnessing to this open and visible miracle.

I have not attempted to deal with the difficulties, some real, and some manufactured by men, that can be found in Scripture. I have only tried in this chapter to set out some of the basic reasons why we can accept the Bible as the Word of God, and use it to our great spiritual comfort.

Jesus revealed his respect for the Old Testament and his belief in its authority by constantly quoting from its pages, and building on its principles in his ministry and teaching. In Luke 4 he explains the Messianic prophecy of Isaiah 61:1–2 concerning Christ's earthly ministry, referring it to himself: "Today, this Scripture has been fulfilled in your hearing" (Luke 4:21) and then promises to work it out in evangelism, healing, and pastoral care. Near the close of his ministry, he celebrates the Passover meal, and uses it to establish the sacrament of the Last Supper, or the Eucharist, within this Biblical context. He makes certain that the disciples will understand the sacrificial and sin-bearing nature of his coming death by direct reference to the promises of Isaiah 53. (See Luke 22:37 and Isa. 53:6.)

After Pentecost, Peter preaching into the teeth of the opponents who had led Jesus to crucifixion, and only a few paces from the mute, but powerful contemporary witness of the empty tomb, explained the death and Resurrection of Jesus, by direct reference to the Risen Lord Jesus.

"This Jesus, delivered up according to the definite plan and foreknowledge of God, you crucified and killed by the hands of lawless men. But God raised him up, having loosed the pangs of death, because it was not possible for him to be held by it." Peter returns to Bible exposition. "For David says concerning him, 'I saw the Lord always before me, for he is at my right hand that I may not be shaken; therefore my heart was glad, and my tongue rejoiced; moreover my flesh will dwell in hope. For thou wilt not abandon my soul to Hades, nor let thy Holy One see corruption. Thou has made known to me the ways of life; thou wilt make me full of gladness with thy presence.'"

Peter in his practical and compelling way continues:

Brethren, may I say to you confidently of the patriarch David that he both died and was buried, and his tomb is with us to this day. Being therefore a prophet, and knowing that God had sworn an oath with him that he would set one of his descendants upon his throne, he foresaw and spoke of the resurrection of the Christ, that he was not abandoned to Hades, nor did his flesh see corruption. This Jesus God raised up, and of that we are all witnesses.

(Acts 2:29–32.)

As bishops, the Bible is solemnly placed in our hands at our consecration. Long before that day we must pray and ponder whether this same action years before when we were made priests expresses outwardly our inward desire above all else as a chief pastor of the flock, and an under-shepherd of Christ the Good Shepherd. Do we desire, as bishops, constantly to open, expound and apply the Old and New Testament Scriptures, in public preaching and private admonition, and, to quote the Prayer Book charge to priests, "and seeing that you cannot by any other means compass the doing of so weighty a work, pertaining to the salvation of man, but with doctrine and exhortation taken out of the holy Scriptures, and with a life agreeable to the same" so "consider how studious ye ought to be in reading and learning the Scriptures . . ."

Bishop Jenkins seems to cast doubt on the moral integrity of Peter and his fellow apostolic witnesses, when he seems unable to affirm the miracle of the bodily Resurrection of Jesus "on the third day", which in his Pentecost sermon Peter clearly states, so that "his flesh did not see corruption". But Bishop Jenkins suggested in his Easter letter (see p. 26) that the most rational explanation for the empty tomb is that the disciples "stole the body". But the inevitable consequences of such an explanation is to cast doubt on the integrity and honesty of the apostolic witnesses; to deny the revealed truth of Holy Scripture that "God raised him from the dead"; and therefore to deny the very miracle of miracles that Christ conquered sin and death and decay, and was raised incorruptible, yet with a visible continuity of likeness with his human body. "Put your finger here, Thomas, and see my hands" (John 20:27) was the answer when Thomas asked to see the nail-marks from Calvary. Dr. Jenkins, with a sad honesty, says: "I cannot conceal or cheat on this, because the whole matter is too important for cheating or concealment, or pretending to particular beliefs that one does not find sufficient reason for holding."

There are historic facts about Jesus Christ which are revealed in the Bible, and are inextricably linked with miracle, which C. S. Lewis defines in his book *Miracles*, as "an interference with Nature by Supernatural power". Perhaps more fully we may speak of miracle as a self-revelatory act of God, which may go beyond God's regular laws of nature, and also in John's Gospel is seen as a "sign from God" (John 2:11).

Certainly, miracle is part of God's pattern of activity, in relation to his Son Jesus Christ, revealed in the Bible. Clearly Dr. Jenkins finds these miracles in the Bible in their plain sense hard to accept. I have come slowly to believe, however, that if a man has deep reservations about the miracles revealed in the Bible concerning the unique birth, death and visible Resurrection of Christ from the open and empty tomb, he should not exercise the office of a bishop in the Church (see p. 26).

Understanding the Faith is not simply a matter of intellectual capability, however. The Divine Author, who as the timeless Holy Spirit of God inbreathed the various and very different authors of the Bible, is the same powerful Holy Spirit, who is the Interpreter to us as we read its pages. Paul put it this way:

> But as it is written, "What no eye has seen, nor ear heard, nor the heart of man conceived, what God has prepared for those who love him," God has revealed to us through the Spirit. For the Spirit searches everything, even the depths of God. For what person knows a man's thoughts except the spirit of the man which is in him? So also no one comprehends the thoughts of God except the Spirit of God. Now we have received not the spirit of the world, but the Spirit which is from God, that we might understand the gifts bestowed on us by God.

> (1 Cor. 2:9–12)

Why do some Christians seem to find it difficult to believe the great historic doctrines of the Creed, and of the Universal Church, thus distressing others, and confusing themselves? Is it because they cannot believe in the great principle of revelation which underlies Scripture, and the principle of the supernatural activity of God, in his own sovereign will, which underlies the unique historic facts of the birth, life, death, Resurrection and Ascension of our Lord Jesus Christ? Yet the summary in the Eucharistic Prayers of the Alternative Services Book surely demands such a belief, when we say:

> Christ *has* died
> Christ *is* risen
> Christ *will* come again.

The Bible was placed in my hands by Archbishop Fisher at my priesting in 1941, and again by Archbishop Ramsey at my consecration in 1971, both in St. Paul's Cathedral. I have come to believe in the Bible's authority, to understand a little of its central message in Christ, and to love its pages more and more in this period of my Christian service, and I recommend it today with ever greater assurance as God's Word to modern man. May each day of your life be an Emmaus walk, as Christ goes with you, opening your eyes to the wonder of the Holy Scriptures, as they centre in him. (See Luke 24:13–35.)

Whenever we read the Bible, we can start by depending on God to reveal its meaning to us, and so we will finish this chapter on the Bible, by adding in the Old Prayer Book Version, the Collect for the Second Sunday in Advent.

Blessed Lord, who hast caused all Holy Scriptures to be written for our learning; grant that we may in such wise hear them, read, mark, learn, and inwardly digest them, that by patience and comfort of thy holy Word, we may embrace and ever hold fast the blessed hope of everlasting life which thou has given us in our Saviour Jesus Christ. Amen.

10

HOW CAN I UNDERSTAND THE EASTER STORY?

Flying in from England, I discovered that Jerusalem was still a Golden City today, as it stands, sun-baked and gleaming, on a hill-top ridge, but surrounded beyond its encircling valleys by the further hills of Judea. Here shepherds still seek for green pastures among the dry scrub and outcrop of the prevailing limestone, while their sheep follow them. This was Mount Zion, where Solomon built his first great Temple from material gathered together by his father David. Here, Nehemiah, working by day and watching by night, gradually rebuilt the House of God after the Exile. Within was the Holy of Holies, cut off from the Holy Place by a great curtain, or veil. It contained the golden mercy-seat, above which the Cherubim, with outstretched wings, stood sentinel, appearing to gaze down upon the mercy-seat, where the blood of the sacrificial lamb was annually brought.

Herod's magnificent Temple, with all the glory of some restored St. Paul's Cathedral, stood here in the days of Jesus the Carpenter, and along this ridge of Mount Zion, or Mount Moriah (2 Chronicles 3:1), he was to be led towards the little hill of Calvary, called Golgotha, or the Hill of the Skull, to die.

It was in this cradle of Jewish history that Jesus was killed, where the three great cultures of Roman law, Jewish religion, and Greek philosophy were seen to meet, symbolically, in the accusation nailed above him on the Cross, "in letters of Greek, and Latin and Hebrew" (Luke 23:38).

Jerusalem has a timeless quality about it, and has changed little down the wide centuries. I remember standing at the busy, noisy bus station in Jerusalem; just above it stands the little hill called "Gordon's Calvary", where the hill, bare and skull-shaped, has great pits, like eyes and nose and mouth, and beside it is the Garden Tomb, with its fine Christian custodian. Whether the body of Jesus was laid here, or in the more traditional place within the great Church of the Holy Sepulchre, matters less than the undoubted historic fact that within a few hundred yards of the site of the ancient Temple courtyard, Jesus was nailed to the Cross on the first Good Friday and then reverently laid dead in the cold stone tomb of the rich and courageous Joseph of Arimathea (John 19: 38–42).

Why write so much history and geography? Because the birth, death and Resurrection of Jesus are the historic facts upon which the Christian Faith stands four-square today still. Secondly, because the geographical and contemporary surroundings of his death help to highlight the overwhelming importance of the historic fact of his sufferings.

Historically, there is no doubt that the Carpenter of Nazareth, Jesus by name, truly lived and really died. Apart from the wealth of Biblical evidence which even the most prejudiced non-Christian can hardly sweep away in its entirety, the fact of the Church in history springs from the life of the Christ of history. In addition, Tacitus and Pliny for the Romans, and Josephus the historian for the Jews, who was certainly no friend of the early Christians, wrote of the fact that Jesus truly lived. That he rose again from the dead is the joyous claim of the Christian Church.

History and geography; Old Testament prophecy and New Testament preaching; the recorded words of Jesus, and the clear and harmonious teaching of the Gospels; the time of his death, and the seeming coincidences surrounding both his death and Resurrection: all these emphasise in progressive measure the extreme importance of his death and Resurrection, and the consequences for all mankind that flow from the darkness and agony and triumph of the Calvary.

Christ died, that he might fulfil Old Testament prophecy

His cruel, bloodstained death, with hands, side and feet pierced, and with his forehead torn by the gashing crown of thorns was not just an unexplained tragedy, or a tragic miscarriage of justice. God did care, and suffered with and in his precious only Son. As Dorothy Sayers wrote, in her comment on the world's sin and cruelty, "at Calvary God at least took his own medicine."

The first coming of Christ, the Anointed One, was to be in humility rather than power. On the foal of an ass, the symbol of peace (rather than the horse, of war), he rode into the city on Palm Sunday. With a towel, the symbol of humble service, he washed the disciples' feet on Maundy Thursday; and stripped of all possessions, the symbol of utter poverty, he hung in naked majesty on the central one of the criminals' gibbets. So low did he stoop, before he could reach us poor sinners. His humanity highlights our proud sinfulness. The ground is surely level around the Cross. In lowliness, as the Suffering Servant of Isaiah's majestic Messianic prophecies, he was also King of Kings, come to reign from his throne upon the Tree.

The Suffering Servant was also to be the Sin-bearer, not only of the people of Israel, but also of the world. "And Nations shall come to your light, and kings to the brightness of your rising" (Isaiah 60:3) is the parallel theme in the later chapters of Isaiah's prophecy.

Christ explained the purpose of his death before he suffered

The cautious doubter could charge the Christian with being wise after the event, and reading back into the Old Testament writings meanings that were not truly there. However, Christ made explicit references to his coming death in four particular ways.

His explanation in preaching

Christ aimed to get two main facts implanted in the disciples' hearts before he suffered; first, who he was, and second, what he came to do, and he would not explain the second until he had established the first. Christian stability today still depends on clearly understanding that Jesus is the Christ, the incarnate Son of God, and that he came to be the Saviour of the world. The Person and work of Christ are fundamental to a firm and assured Christian faith. (See again Chapter 8.)

Jesus said, "Who do you say that I am?" Peter answered him, "You are the Christ." "And he began to teach them that the Son of man must suffer many things . . . and be killed, and after three days rise again" (Mark 8:29–31). After this first explanation, he returns to the theme of his death and the Resurrection regularly (Mark 8:31–38; 9:9; 9:30–32; 10:32–34; etc). Here, he was establishing the fact of his death and the promise of his Resurrection, as something expected by himself, understood by Moses and Elijah in the mysterious moment of Transfiguration (Luke 9:31) and allowed by God, so that it might become the gateway of blessing to all believers (John 19:10, 11). Christ's constant repetition of warning and hope shows that the death of Christ was "meant" to happen. God was ultimately in control, "for the Son of Man also came not to be served but to serve, and to give his life as a ransom for many" (Mark 10:45).

His explanation of prophecy

The whole chapter of Isaiah 53 tells of the Shepherd Saviour who will carry the sins of his people, and die in their place, bearing their penalty.

"All we like sheep have gone astray; we have turned every one to his own way; and the Lord has laid on him the iniquity of us all" (v. 3, 6). On the very eve of his death, he quoted from Isaiah 53 saying, "For I tell you that this scripture must be fulfilled in me," "And he was reckoned with transgressors" (Isa. 53:12 and Luke 22:37). On the Cross he took Psalm 22 upon his lips, with its detailed prophecies of spiritual (v. 1–3), mental (v. 6–11) and physical suffering (v. 14–18) (Matthew 27:43–46 and John 19:23, 24, 28).

Jesus went to great lengths to show by his preaching that the Scripture expected Christ, when he came, to suffer, and that this was all foreordained by God, and known to Jesus. The ultimate triumph of Resurrection was also assured. By his use of Biblical prophecy, he both explained that he himself was the Suffering Servant of Isaiah, and also showed that he would die in the place of others, bearing their sins in his own body on the tree (1 Peter 2:24; another passage referring clearly to Isaiah 53).

His explanation in the Passover Service

The identification of the suffering, sin-bearing Saviour with the Passover Lamb, and the "coincidence", so called, of Christ's death coming at Passover time, re-emphasised these first two points. To the Twelve, Jesus now speaks in utterly frank terms. Like the Passover Lamb, perfect, harmless and unresisting, he too goes forward to his Cross, leaving the symbols of broken bread and out-poured wine to assure us, in every coming generation, that in love his body was broken for us, and in the shedding of his very life's blood, he gave himself for us. He took our place by dying instead of us while bearing the penalty of our sins; for he alone could pay this penalty. He died our death, "and the Lord has laid on him the iniquity of us all" (Isa. 53:6; Luke 24:44–48). At last John the Baptist's mysterious cry, reminiscent of Isaiah's prophecy, which had heralded his coming, was now fully understood in his death. "Behold the Lamb of God, who takes away the sin of the world!" (John 1:29). In the setting of all the ritual and doctrine surrounding the annual Passover memorial of the deliverance of the Israelites from death and slavery, Jesus said plainly, "This is my blood of the covenant,

which is poured out for many for the forgiveness of sins"
(Matt. 26:28).

*His explanation of the sign of the Temple, to be destroyed
and raised*

Here conservative scholars and liberal scholars face serious
disagreement, highlighted by a letter to *The Times*, after
Easter Day 1985.

"Once again this Easter," writes Canon Alan Wilkinson,
"the lectionary of the Church of England has bidden us
re-read the stories of the Exodus" (the deliverance of the
Jews under Moses' leadership, from Pharaoh's tyranny in
Egypt), "at both the Eucharist and the daily offices. We
have sung hymns which depict the Crucifixion and Resurrection of Jesus in terms of the Passover celebration of the
Exodus, which was also the context of the Last Supper. A
hundred years ago, most Christians would have regarded
the Exodus stories as "plain historical fact" – i.e. that
is what *we* would have seen and experienced if we had
been present. We now realise that we cannot separate
'what happens' from the cultural pre-suppositions of the
participants."

Canon Wilkinson now makes an extraordinary leap of
logic. Having disposed of the "plain historical fact" of the
Passover in the teeth of the Old Testament, and the
ancient teachings of the Jewish Faith, and the teaching of
Christ about the establishment of the Christian Eucharist
developing from the Passover meal in the Gospels we are
"to be agnostic about 'what happened' at the Exodus".

What are we to make of the Exodus? He suggests "we
miss the point completely" unless "we treat the Exodus
stories as of great symbolic power which abound in rich,
poetic, personal and political significance."

His philosophical argument of "religious significance,
but not historical fact" is a logical progression from
Bishop David Jenkins' statement. "The Resurrection of
Jesus from the dead is the assertion, made by God and
received by faith, that in this world, through this world,

and beyond this world we may be sure that, in the end, love succeeds, love brings it off; love has the last word" ("The Meaning of Easter", *The Durham Lamp*, 1985). Beautiful words they are, but the bishop continues, "But we do not know this because the grave of Jesus was empty. Maybe it was, maybe it was *not*. As is now perhaps, alas, notorious, *I personally do not know whether the grave was empty or not*" (my italics). I refer more fully to this statement in Chapter 11 on miracles.

Canon Wilkinson continues: "Yet the Exodus stories *dominate* the Old Testament and the Jewish faith, as the Resurrection *dominates* the New Testament and the Christian faith."

His "religious significance without historical fact", which appears to be also Bishop Jenkins' philosophical approach, reaches its inevitable unsure climax, when he writes: "If it is allowable to treat the Exodus stories in this manner, why is it illegitimate to treat the Resurrection stories similarly? We simply cannot know what we would have seen and experienced at the tomb, or in the Upper Room."

But over against these shadowy areas of doubt and speculation, Jesus himself used a symbol of such power that even his enemies turned it against him at his trial, remembered it on the very night he died, and found Peter proclaiming it after the miracle of his Easter Day Resurrection, in his Pentecost sermon.

The Jews then said to him, "What sign have you to show us for doing this?" (the cleansing of the Temple in John 2:13–17) Jesus answered them: "Destroy this temple, and in three days, I will raise it up." The Jews then said, "It has taken forty-six years to build this temple, and will you raise it up in three days? But he spoke of the temple of his body. When therefore he was raised from the dead, his disciples remembered that he had said this: and they believed the word which Jesus had spoken" (John 2:18–22).

Here was powerful symbol based upon historic fact, first his own death and Resurrection "on the third day", and finally and symbolically the sack of Jerusalem in AD 70, the destruction of the Temple, and yet by that time the establishment of Christ's body the Church. But we have no authority to reject the historical core of the Christian revelation, by an unwillingness to believe the sheer miracle of the historical Resurrection of Christ "on the third day", by immediately allegorising a vivid sign and by passing over the historic fact, which the Sign portrays. The two words "miracle" and "sign" are interchangeable words in John's Gospel (see John 2:11) for they are given to show forth Christ's glory, and to elicit faith in Christ's person, as the Son of God.

Christ promised that the New Testament writers would fully explain his death and Resurrection

Jesus promised his Apostles that the Father would send the Holy Spirit, to do through them what he had done through the Old Testament writers, namely to reveal clear truth which could be preserved in written words. The Holy Spirit would "bring to your remembrance all that I have said to you" (John 14:26); he would "teach you all things" (v. 26 again); and "he will declare to you the things that are to come" (John 16:13). Thus, Gospels, Epistles and prophecies in the New Testament would have the mark of Divine authorship upon them.

To the disciples walking to Emmaus, Jesus had revealed that he himself was the Messiah at the centre of Scripture (Luke 24:25–27), and on the same Easter day explained that his coming must be seen in terms of death and resurrection; of the preaching of the Cross and the conversion of sinners; and of the need to keep the Person and work of Jesus at the centre of their thinking and speaking (Luke 24:45–48). We find in Scripture that we are sinners, needing the forgiveness of our sins (1 Cor. 15:1–9); we are rebels, needing to surrender and find peace with God (Rom. 4:24; 5:11); we are self-willed sheep, for whom the Good Shepherd died (1 Pet. 2:21–25), and to whom we must therefore return in penitence; we are lost, and needing to be found (Luke 15:1–7); we are unclean, needing to be fully cleansed (1 John 1:7; 2:2); we are outcasts, needing to be made sons of God (Rom. 8:9–17; Gal. 4:4–7); we deserve the punishment that leads to Hell, but we can, through Christ's death, receive pardon and righteousness that leads to Heaven. No wonder we sing:

> Bearing shame and scoffing rude
> In my place, condemned, He stood.
> Sealed my pardon with His blood,
> Alleluia, what a Saviour!

No wonder, also, when we look up into Christ's face, as in imagination we see him hanging on the Cross, we recognise both his love and faith, as we cry:

> Were the whole realm of nature mine,
> That were an offering far too small,
> Love so amazing, so divine,
> Demands my soul, my life, my all.

If this had been the end, however, we should never have been sure that his death had secured our pardon, his life-blood had paid the penalty for our sins, or that the Cross was a victory, although it looked like a defeat. Good Friday led to Easter Day; the Cross and Tomb led to a Garden in the sunshine of the dawn; and the dying Sin-bearer arose to be the living and life-giving Saviour.

On what grounds can we believe that the Resurrection truly took place, and what results follow from this historic fact? The present-day controversies about the empty tomb, the body of Jesus, the trustworthiness of the Christian witnesses, and the integrity of Peter's character as he preached that on the third day, Christ Jesus rose, alive, from the tomb, are *not* issues of distant academic interest. They affect the integrity of us present-day clergy, the assurance of our preaching concerning forgiveness and eternal life, and the confidence with which our people can depend on the Gospel we are pledged at our ordination to proclaim, for their salvation.

The reasons for belief in the Resurrection of Christ

There are three traditional reasons, to which due weight must always be given.

a) Every Easter the whole Church of Christ proclaims that Christ was raised from the dead, and every Sunday millions of Christians say in the Apostles' Creed, "I believe in Jesus Christ, who was crucified, dead and buried, he descended into Hell (or Hades); the third day he rose again from the dead."

Here is a living tradition of 2,000 years, which cannot easily be overthrown by the openly expressed doubts of this historic authenticity, by Bishop Hensley Henson of Hereford and then of Durham in the 1910's; by Bishop Barnes of Birmingham in the 1920s, or by Bishop Jenkins, of Durham in the 1980s, even though three times in this century the Church of England has had to contend with three bishops who in differing ways publicly expressed their doubts. Although doubts wither, and truth conquers, it is still necessary to assert the historic truths of the Christian Faith in each generation, and the Easter miracle is still at the heart of the living Christian community of all the contemporary churches.

b) The Church of England teaches the reality of the Resurrection. Article 4 of the 39 Articles says, "Christ did truly rise again from death, and took again his body, with flesh, bones, and all things appertaining to the perfection of man's nature."

We do not just believe in the resuscitation of the corpse. When Jesus conquered death by raising Lazarus, it was to his former life, and he would have died again, even though in that act of power he taught that he was "the resurrection and the life", and that through faith in him, we find eternal life (1 Cor. 15:50) but we shall inherit a "spiritual body" (1 Cor. 15:44) and "the flesh and *bones* and all things appertaining to the perfection of man's nature" is how the Church defines our resurrection bodies, which will be recognisable but transformed, as Christ's body was like, but changed.

Dr. John Stott, Director of the London Institute for Contemporary Christian Studies ("Reflections on the Resurrection": *The Times*, April 1985), says of the bodily resurrection of Christ that "on the third day" bore "witness to a dated event" and makes me wonder how Dr. David Jenkins in the now famous *Credo* programme could have said that, even from reading Paul in 1 Corinthians, it did not seem to him that "there was any *one* event which you could identify with the Resurrection, only a series of experiences."

The Church of England takes what at first reading may seem to be a small detail, "on the third day", and holds to it with tenacity, in the Apostle's Creed, and in the Nicene Creed, building on Paul's explicit statement in 1 Corinthians 15:3–4, which he claims "he received", and which Jesus promised on a number of occasions (cf. John 2:19 and Luke 9:22). This was the miraculous event that took place on the first Easter Day, when the stone was rolled away, the tomb in Joseph of Arimathea's garden was found to be empty, and Christ met with his startled disciples, truly risen from the dead.

It will not do for a bishop of the Church of England to say that "we do *not* know this because the grave of Jesus was empty. *I do not know whether the grave was empty or not*. The evidence of the texts, the nature of the tradition, and the general facts about the way people all over the world rapidly believe appropriate stories to support their religious beliefs, leave me *wholly uncertain* (my italics) about the Empty Tomb as literal historic fact." (*The Durham Lamp*)

If in the past Professor Jenkins said that in a secular university to students, he would presumably have been responsible to the Board of Divinity in which he lectured to substantiate his speculations. Today he bears the heavy responsibility of being a diocesan bishop of the Church of

England, of making such a negative statement of unbelief, when he is by his very consecration as a bishop and father in God to his clergy and people a guardian of the Faith as the Church of England has received that Faith, and proclaims these truths. I return to this issue later, in the chapter on miracles, in a fuller way, but Chapter 8 "Between Sunset and Dawn" in Frank Morison's classic *Who Moved the Stone*? in a scholarly way explores the seven possible "rational" explanations for the empty tomb. He considered Dr. Jenkins' suggestion as the least, not the most plausible. "I do not propose to devote any considerable space to testing the historical accuracy of this charge, because the verdict has been anticipated by the almost universal sense and feeling of mankind. So far as I know there is not a single writer whose work is of critical value today who holds (this view) . . . Even if it had been possible and the disciples the men to do it, the subsequent history of Christianity would have been different. Sooner or later someone who knew the facts would have 'split'. Further, no great moral structure like the Early Church, based as it was upon lifelong persecution and personal suffering, could have reared its head upon a statement which every one of the eleven apostles knew to be a lie" (p. 89).

Quietly Morison disposes of the "rational" explanations, and returns inexorably and very persuasively to the historical miracle that "on the third day, he rose again" and in such a regenerated physical way, as taught in the Bible, and the 39 Articles.

c) The Bible reveals the Resurrection as the undisputed climax of each of the Gospel stories. The *consensus fidelium* down the wide centuries of time is not easily overthrown. To depart from the historic fact of Christ's birth, life, miracles, death, Resurrection, Ascension, and Return, is to try to build a religion only on ideas that Jesus suggested. This produces but a frail humanism, without the "earthy" quality of the historic fact of Jesus of Nazareth, Carpenter as well as Christ; Sin-bearer as well as Teacher; Risen Lord as well as Healer; both Very God and Very Man. As Lord Ramsey, former Archbishop of

Canterbury, writes, "It is a desperate procedure to try and build a Christian gospel upon the words of Jesus of Galilee, apart from the climax of Calvary, Easter and Pentecost . . . Life-through-death is the principle of Jesus's whole life; so utterly new and foreign to the expectations of man was this doctrine, that only historical events could have created it" (*The Resurrection of Christ*, Bles). Alan Richardson says, "Against all modern attempts to explain the Resurrection as something natural and comprehensible, it is necessary to insist that the Resurrection of Jesus is miracle, mysterious and irreducible, from the biblical point of view" (p. 194, *A Theological Word Book*).

The fulness of the Christian Faith cannot be just pulped through a child's sieve to make it a boneless mash suitable for modern man. The miracle of the Resurrection has been called "the best attested fact of history" and there is plenty of carefully reasoned evidence to support this claim. I can remember preaching on this great subject in St. Paul's Cathedral on Easter Day, and suggesting that people who had either intellectual doubts about the Resurrection, or wanted to find Christ as their own Saviour, should meet at the Great West Door of the Cathedral where the then Dean and Chapter had erected a beautiful "Easter Garden". It was a moving experience to offer booklets on personal faith to men and women of different ages and from many countries and continents, who were visiting London at that time. I also remember a businessman asking me for a book for deeper study and being ready to recommend to him *Who Moved the Stone?* by Frank Morison (published by Send the Light Trust), mentioned above; *The Evidences for the Resurrection*, by Professor Sir Norman Anderson (Inter-Varsity); *Miracles* by C. S. Lewis (Fontana); and *The Resurrection of Christ*, by A. M. Ramsey. I was reminded by the variety of people I spoke to on that occasion that the Cross is for all men everywhere, and that Christ who rose from the dead at Eastertime came back from death as the Saviour of the whole world, and not just of one class or one nation. For those who have intellectual difficulties these books might well help, and I would add John Wenham's more recent book *Easter Enigma* which is in the same "genre" as Morison, but tackles apparent diversities in the texts with positive thoroughness, and is a fine example of harmonising rather than destructive criticism.

Because I have been critical of Dr. Jenkins' rejection of belief in the "Empty Tomb" as literal historic fact and also because I know from letters to me that many people have been disturbed in their faith, I add here three selective reasons of a rational sort to undergird the clear Biblical statements about Christ's Resurrection on Easter morning. Faith is not blind credulity: it is reasonable, but it is based on facts plainly set out in Scripture. God gives us minds, which as we study the Scriptures can be illuminated by the Holy Spirit, to understand the facts. Here are three reasonable ideas, amongst others, to help assure us that the Empty Tomb was literal historical fact. I return to this issue more fully in the next chapter.

i) Christ's enemies could not produce the dead body which would have immediately refuted the disciples' claims that Jesus was risen from the dead. However, they did the best they could. They manufactured a lie, as hastily as possible. Already, the chief priests and Pharisees had hurried to Pontius Pilate the Governor, fearing now Jesus was evidently dead, that the disciples would steal his body and proclaim him alive again, so they said to Pilate (See Matthew 27:62–66):

> "Sir, we remember how that impostor said, while he was still alive, 'After three days I will rise again.' Therefore order the sepulchre to be made secure until the third day, lest his disciples go and steal him away, and tell the people 'He has risen from the dead,' and the last fraud will be worse than the first." Pilate said to them, "You have a guard of soldiers; go make it as secure as you can." So they went and made the sepulchre secure, by sealing the stone, and setting a guard.

ii) Christ's friends were so slow to believe (even Thomas for whom a whole week passed before he came to faith), that we see the Resurrection as a fact which they could not finally deny, rather than a figment of imagination at which they immediately grasped. This was no despairing story desperately made up to hide unpalatable facts. This was an overwhelming truth breaking into their sorrow and sadness with mighty assurance, as they met with the living Christ.

iii) Look also at the coincidences of Eastertime by studying the relevant passages in the Gospels for yourself. He died on the eve of the Sabbath, thus restricting the movement of any who would seek to steal his body away. He was laid in a rich man's tomb, thus ensuring all possible safety against theft. The seal placed upon the stone and the round-the-clock military guard provided total security against the despoiling of the tomb either in secret or by a strong body of men. These simple facts cut off any alternative theories about either body-snatching or secret resuscitation, and point to the truth of Scripture, as proclaimed by Peter in his Pentecost Sermon (Acts 2:23). "This Jesus, you crucified and killed . . . God raised him up having loosed the pangs of death, because it was not possible for him to be held by it." The Christian Faith stands upon this ground of historical events, a clear platform for an assured step of personal faith and committal. This inability of his enemies to produce the body of Christ; the slowness of the disciples to believe; and the God-ordained coincidences, as they must have first seemed to be, are only three of the strands, starting on Easter Day itself, which were woven, during the great forty days from Easter to Ascension, into the tapestry of the assured victory of Christ, the King of Kings.

The results of the miracle of the Resurrection

Jesus took infinite pains to prepare his disciples not only for a true and deep understanding of his Cross, as set out earlier in this chapter, but by emphasising that the Resurrection was the natural and God-ordained corollary to his suffering on Calvary. Jesus emphasised that his death was true to the prophecies of Scripture; that it was the expected gateway through which he should pass to his triumph; and that his death would so certainly be followed by his Resurrection that he seldom taught about his death without a reference to his rising again. "The Son of man must suffer many things . . . and be killed, and after three days rise again" (Mark 8:31). "And as they were coming down the mountain (of Transfiguration) and he charged them to tell no one what they had seen, until the Son of man should have risen from the dead" (Mark 9:9). "Jesus was teaching his disciples, saying to them, 'The Son of man will be delivered into the hands of men, and they will kill him; and when he is killed, after three days he will rise.' But they did not understand the saying, and they were afraid to ask him" (Mark 9:31–32). Despite their dullness of understanding, he persisted in this teaching. "And taking the twelve again, he began to tell them what was to happen to him, saying, 'Behold, we are going up to Jerusalem; and the Son of man will be delivered to the chief priests and the scribes; and they will condemn him to death . . . and they will mock him, and spit upon him, and scourge him and kill him; and after three days he will arise'" (Mark 10:32–34). By demonstrating his detailed foreknowledge of both his suffering and his subsequent triumph, he prepared them fully to understand the glory of Easter when finally the fact happened as he said. Three results of the miracle of the Resurrection can be noted here:

The endorsement of Christ's divine claims

Jesus said that he himself would rise again, and the Scriptures had said that the Christ, the Anointed One, would rise again. Jesus quoted from the Messianic psalm (Psalm 16): "For thou does not give me up to Sheol, or let thy godly one see the Pit. Thou dost show me the path of life; in thy

presence there is fullness of joy, in thy right hand are
pleasures for evermore" (v. 10–11).

Peter after Pentecost picks up this Christ-authorised
prophecy with joy, and uses it in his first great sermon
(Acts 2:25–31). Notice the phrase "David's tomb is with
us to this day" (v. 29) with the obvious allusion the opposition would have seen with chagrin, that the open tomb of
Jesus was empty, for "David foresaw and spoke of the
Resurrection of the Christ, that he was not abandoned to
Hades, nor did his flesh see corruption" (v. 31). Here is a
clear statement of Jesus' *physical* Resurrection, and Peter
continues, "This Jesus God raised up, and of that we all
are witnesses" (v. 32).

On the road to Emmaus on the first Easter Day he
explained to his two mystified disciples that the things that
happened to their friend, Jesus of Nazareth, on Good
Friday, were the very things that should have happened to
the Christ, the Son of the Living God. "And Jesus said to
them, 'Oh foolish men and slow of heart to believe all that
the prophets have spoken! Was it not necessary that *the
Christ* should suffer these things and enter into his glory?'
And beginning with Moses and all the prophets, he interpreted to them in all the Scriptures the *things concerning
himself*" (Luke 24:25–27). In this way he sought to bring
into focus the things they knew had happened to Jesus and
the things the Scriptures said would happen to the Christ.
The fact that God raised Jesus from the dead shows how
his claim to be the Son of God was true. It is the very
God-Man himself with whom we may company through
life. With Mary Magdalene in faith, we may cry, "I have
seen the Lord."

As Dr. John Stott puts it, "It seems clear that the
apostles saw the Resurrection as the decisive, divine
reversal of the human verdict which had been passed on
Jesus by his condemnation and execution . . . moreover,
given the verdict had been public, its reversal needed to
be public too and so Mary's joyful cry was theologically
true, as well as heart-warmingly sure: 'I have seen the
LORD.'"

The efficacy of Christ's atoning death

Archbishop Michael Ramsey wrote, "The many references to the fulfilment of prophecy declare that here is no haphazard disaster, but a divine act of redemption. On the Cross Jesus is King. The Crucifixion is not a defeat, needing the Resurrection to reverse it, but a victory, which the Resurrection quickly follows and seals." "His death is a divine act of Redemption," continues the archbishop. To understand this we do well to study a variety of Scriptural references of which these are a selection:

Peter wrote: "Christ suffered for you, and he himself bore (or carried up) our sins in his body on the tree . . . By his wounds you have been healed" (1 Peter 2:21, 24). Quoting from the fifty-third chapter of Isaiah, Paul wrote, "Jesus our Lord, who was put to death for our trespasses and raised for our justification. Therefore, since we are justified by faith, we have peace with God through our Lord Jesus Christ" (Rom. 4:25; 5:1).

On Maundy Thursday the Lord Jesus took bread, blessed God his Father, gave thanks and broke and gave them the bread with the cup, saying, "Do this in remembrance of me" (Luke 22:19) and "This is my blood of the covenant, which is poured out for many for the forgiveness of sins" (Matthew 26:28). As P. T. Forsyth put it in his book, *The Work of Christ*, "Easter proclaims that the Cross is where the centre of gravity of the Gospel lies." We dare move away from Calvary and the open tomb, therefore, only at the danger of spiritual poverty.

Now, in the Alternative Service Book, at the Eucharist the whole congregation confidently cry, "Christ has died; Christ is risen; Christ will come again." When I preached on Easter Day in Norwich Cathedral for the last time as diocesan bishop I shall long remember that cry in our packed cathedral. At the end of the sermon we said together the ancient Easter dialogue: "Christ is risen: He is risen indeed," and then we called out "Alleluia, Alleluia, Alleluia", each one louder that the last. When all the discussions are over the truth remains: "He is risen" and in his conquest over sin, and death, we find the assurance of pardon and eternal life. Alleluia, Praise the Lord, indeed!

The evangelisation of Christ's world

This is Christ's world. He was the agent of God the Father's creative activity. "For in him all things were created . . . He is before all things, and in him all things hold together" (Col. 1:16–17). He is also the agent of God's re-creative work within men's hearts. As soon as the Lord Jesus Christ indwelt the Apostles by his Spirit on the Day of Pentecost, they preached every day that Christ was risen; they showed forth his death each week in the breaking of the bread on the Lord's Day; the Sabbath of the Jews soon became the Sunday of the Christians, and remains one more testimony to the events of the first Easter Day; and the ministry both of Word and Sacrament has its special meaning and power because both centre in the living, loving, dying, and risen Lord Jesus.

It would have been ethically impossible for the disciples to have preached a lie, and yet lived such blameless lives, if Christ had not risen from the dead; and it would have been psychologically unbearable to have been partakers of the broken bread and outpoured wine week after week, if in fact his body was decaying in a tomb, and he was not alive for evermore. Of *course* he was alive! They *knew* him, and he had begun to transform their lives by his indwelling Spirit and power, so that their testimony to his presence reinforced their preaching of his Cross. For the Christian every Breaking of Bread is a true Eucharist of praise and thanksgiving, of remembrance and hope, and of strong assurance that we feed on him by faith, until that great day when he will come again and receive his Church to be with him, and before we all worship him in the glory of Heaven.

All down the wide centuries since the first Easter Day, evangelism, or the winning of men and women to personal and total allegiance to Jesus Christ, has sprung out of the

deep understanding that Christ both died for our sins and
was raised again to justify us. The children in our Sunday
Schools have a mighty victory to celebrate when in one of
their choruses they sing:

> He lives, he lives, Christ Jesus lives today.
> He walks with me, he talks with me,
> along life's narrow way,
> He lives, he lives, Salvation to impart,
> You ask me how I know he lives,
> He lives within my heart!

To summarise, we have seen sound reasons for belief in
the historic fact that Christ Jesus truly rose from the dead
on Easter Day. We have studied together some of the
results of the Resurrection; that Jesus is truly the Son
of God; that in his death he paid the penalty of wrong-
doing and sin; that he gladly died in our place to be our
Sin-bearer; and that this Good News for dying men of a
loving Saviour, and a living Lord, must be proclaimed by
Christ's disciples till the end of time and to the far corners
of the earth. What is our personal reaction to the sacrifice
of Calvary and the glory of Easter Day?

The response to the triumph of the Resurrection

There are two obvious responses to the Easter message,
depending on the present position of the hearer. Some
face a call to service, springing from a renewed love for
Christ. Others face a clear call to personal faith in Christ,
springing from a fresh insight into the Gospel.

The Call to Service

When I was Principal of Oak Hill Theological College, I
was impressed with the quality of our ordinands, and the
depth of their sacrifice, whether it was the sacrifice of
money, of family life, of time or even of life itself. A civil
engineer, having spent much of his savings on the support

of his wife and children during training, now receives a curate's stipend at a third of his previous salary. At least three doctors decided that even with all the opportunities of healing men's minds and bodies, which they had already, they should yet be ordained. Men give up positions of responsibility, trust, and financial security for two or three or more years of ordination training. As C. T. Studd, the England cricketer of an earlier generation, put it, "If Jesus Christ be God and died for me, nothing is too hard for me to do for him."

Evangelism has long-term results. During the ten years of my time as Principal, I discovered that in any one year, never less than ten per cent of our Church of England ordination candidates in training trace their personal conversion to one of Dr. Billy Graham's earlier crusades, and in the fourteen years I have been Bishop of Norwich, clergy of all schools of thought have said the same thing. Already some men have approached us in the diocese about stipendiary and non-stipendiary ordination training, following Dr. Graham's Mission England meetings in Norwich and Ipswich in the summer of 1984. The next paragraph should therefore be approached with caution! Who knows where discipleship can lead?

The Call to Faith

For others the challenge of Easter is a call to personal faith, even though they may have been in church circles for many years. A man said to me recently, "I have been a church-goer all my life, and as my business had taken me travelling I had been churchwarden of at least three separate churches as well as being leader of one of the church's youth organisations in a number of parishes. My worship, however, was curiously empty, until my vicar introduced me to Jesus Christ as Saviour and Lord." The focus of faith is Christ himself. What matters is not the strength of our personal faith but its direction. It must be towards Christ if it is to be effective. Many years ago Bonhoeffer died in a Nazi concentration camp. In his last great book,

Ethics, he wrote, "The foundation of my life is the life, death and resurrection of the Lord Jesus Christ. Faith means the finding and holding fast to this foundation. It means casting anchor upon it and being held fast by it. Faith means founding my life upon a foundation which is outside myself . . . upon an eternal and Holy Foundation, upon Christ. Faith means being held captive by the sight of Jesus Christ." Have you ever personally encountered the Lord Jesus Christ? Each one of us needs to look into his face at Calvary, to see the agony that he suffered for our sins, and in our place, and then to rejoice that he who died to save us now lives to keep us. In the "Comfortable Words" of the old Prayer Book Holy Communion Service Jesus says, "Come to me all who labour and are heavy laden, and I will give you rest" (Matthew 11:28). Because I am writing this book in the final year before I retire from being Bishop of Norwich, I have also been remembering the start of this chapter in the life of my wife and family and myself, fourteen years ago. I finished my Enthronement Sermon with a prayer based upon ancient words of St. Augustine. If this particular chapter on Christ's Cross and Resurrection is helping you at a deeper level to join in the cry which is the title of this book *This is Our Faith*, may I offer it to you, to build it in the treasury of your personal devotional life of prayer, and of Bible-reading?

Lord Jesus my Saviour, let me now come to thee;
My heart is cold; O Lord warm it by thy selfless love.
My heart is sinful: cleanse it by thy precious blood.
My heart is weak; strengthen it by thy Joyous Spirit.
My heart is empty: fill it with thy Divine Presence.
Lord Jesus my heart is thine: possess it always and only
    for thyself. Amen.

To summarise this chapter, what are the great benefits that accrue to man, as a result of Good Friday and Easter Day? Because of Calvary man can be forgiven for his sins; brought into personal relationship with God, as Father; made righteous in his sight, and given eternal life and a place in Heaven for all eternity. Because of Easter Day, man can be sure of Christ's victory over sin, death, judgment and Hell. He can know the friendship of the living Lord Jesus with him, day by day. He can look forward to the hope of inheriting a new and glorified resurrection body one day, so that death loses its final sting. All this becomes his, not through years of weary struggle, but by personal trust and faith in Jesus as Saviour and Lord. No wonder Christians down the years cry "Hallelujah" not only at Eastertime, but at all times!

11

A REASONABLE FAITH
IN MIRACLES

As I listen to Don Cupitt, and read Dr. David Jenkins, and go back to Professor Hick and his colleagues writing in *The Myth of God Incarnate*, I try to enter into the minds of radical writers, to see why they seem to find it hard to believe the doctrines of the Christian Faith, in their plain sense, as seen in the Bible, defined in the Creeds, and taught in the Church by equally clear but more positively believing theologians. The present controversy is not between clever academic theologians and simple parochial preachers. During the first forty years of my ordained ministry, the Church of England was led by Archbishop Geoffrey Fisher, Archbishop Michael Ramsey, and Archbishop Donald Coggan. They had so many First Class Honours to their names, that although broadly they represented Central, High and Evangelical Churchmanship positions, they were theological scholars of eminence, but thoroughly and broadly conservative in their belief in the supernatural quality of the Christian Faith.

Professor Hick's colleague, Michael Goulder (page 55) seeks to avoid the miraculous, by dismissing the supernatural in the life and ministry of Jesus, and especially in His death and resurrection: "We are *not* obliged to accept the first Christians' *supernaturalist* account of what happened; indeed as historians, we shall be bound to prefer a *naturalist* account, if one can be offered . . ."

I believe as present-day Christians, it is reasonable for

us to accept the eternal truths of the supernatural and it is my purpose in this chapter to show how we can so believe, within a reality of revelation, which can transform our lives through the risen Christ.

Peter Mullen, writing in *The Times* under the heading "The Radicals' Flight from Reality", states: "Contemporary theological controversialists such as Don Cupitt and the Bishop of Durham have succeeded in attracting attention to the doctrine of God, and the mode of his action, or lack of it in the world. So Cupitt tells us we must take leave of the consoling idea of providence, and David Jenkins is set against all sorts of miraculous intervention . . ." Jenkins is at odds with Cupitt on the doctrine of God, but both men firmly believe in the idea of human perfectibility. Don Cupitt writes, "The only way to salvation is a decision to live one's life by an absolute standard that requires of us singleness of mind, inner integrity and disinterested love." Mullen comments, "Is that *all*? Who then can be saved?" Jenkins and Cupitt agree perfectly together and they are, historically considered, a recrudescence of Pelagianism, so called after the monk who opposed St. Augustine's teaching on original sin and man's depravity. Pelagianism is a very English disease, which involves the falsely consoling thought that we can pull ourselves up by our own bootstraps. All we need is a singleness of mind . . . inner integrity . . . disinterested love, and so on. But the experience of this century ought to teach us that Pelagianism is a false doctrine, a heresy which needs to be condemned. Paul's psychology is much more accurate, when he tells us that he does the evil he does not want to do, and that he does not do the good that he *would* like to do.

A shallow view of man's sinfulness lulls us into a false hope that a rational religion, without the miracle of God's sovereign intervention, may be enough.

I believe that the procession of miracles concerning the birth, death, Resurrection and Ascension of Jesus, were not only true miracles which are etched upon the tapestry of history, but are the necessary foundations upon which our salvation in time and in eternity depend.

A Reasonable Faith in Miracles

At miracles we must now look, if we are to understand and then grasp that the Christian Faith, and its power dynamically to transform our lives, depends ultimately upon that chapter of miracles which the Church maintains are inextricably related to the historic Person of Jesus of Nazareth.

Forgive me, if I pause on the threshold of this chapter to talk about what miracles are, *sui generis*, because my generation can still remember Professor C. E. M. Joad on the radio, saying, "It all depends what you mean by *miracle*," in an Alice in Wonderland way. If I go too slowly for you at this point, remember that Joad himself came steadily from questioning doubt to Christian faith, so a little definition of our terms is "a good thing"!

Before writing this chapter I have been reading again C. S. Lewis's book, *Miracles – a preliminary study* (Collins: Fontana), which although first published in 1947, when I remember C. S. Lewis at the height of his powers as a don at Oxford, is still, nearly forty years later, a classic in its field. This is because he takes slow but conscientious thinkers seriously, and leads us by the hand, through intellectual labyrinths, to "The Grand Miracle" (chapter 14).

"The central miracle asserted by Christians is the Incarnation. They say that God became man. Every other miracle prepares for this, or exhibits this, or results from this. Just as every *natural* event is the manifestation at a particular place and moment of Nature's total character, so every particular *Christian* miracle manifests at a particular place and moment the character and significance of the Incarnation. There is no question in Christianity of arbitrary interferences just scattered about. It relates not a series of disconnected raids on Nature, but the various steps of a strategically coherent invasion – an invasion which intends complete conquest and 'occupation'."

When I was a young rector of an Oxford city church, this next and most vivid analogy of Christ the diver made a strong impact. So many students, matured by the harrowing events of World War II, had just arrived in Oxford, seeking for a faith that was not only reasonable but

127

life-transforming. I believe that C. S. Lewis made the great miracles of the faith evident and reasonable to serious seekers, and there is a timeless quality in his thought, that can touch our bruised and seeking minds today. In quoting him, I pay my humble tribute to him. Also, I notice that this illustration links the miracle of Incarnation closely with the miracle of the death and Resurrection of Jesus, and I believe there is a cohesion in the miracles *concerning* Christ, which drives us forward to wrestle with "miracles" as such, for I believe our faith is in fact inseparable from miracle.

"In the Christian story God descends to re-ascend. He comes down; down from the heights of absolute being into time and space, down into humanity; down further still, if embryologists are right, to recapitulate in the womb ancient and pre-human phases of life; down to the very roots and sea-bed of the Nature He has created. But He goes down to come up again and bring the whole ruined world up with Him. One has the picture of a strong man stooping lower and lower to get himself underneath some great complicated burden. He must stoop in order to lift, he must also disappear under the load before he incredibly straightens his back and marches off with the whole mass swaying on his shoulders. Or one may think of a diver, first reducing himself to nakedness, then glancing in mid-air, then gone with a splash, vanished, rushing down through green and warm water into black and cold water, down through increasing pressure into the death-like region of ooze and slime and old decay; then up again, back to colour and light, his lungs almost bursting, till suddenly he breaks surface again, holding in his hand the dripping, precious thing that he went down to recover. He and it are both coloured now that they have come up into the light: down below, where it lay colourless in the dark, he lost his colour too . . . Death and Re-birth – go down to go up – it is a key principle. Through this bottleneck, this belittle-ment, the highroad nearly always lies. The doctrine of the Incarnation, if accepted, puts this principle even more emphatically at the centre. The pattern is there in Nature because it was first there in God . . . certainly no seed ever fell from so fair a tree into so dark and cold a soil as would furnish more than a faint analogy to this huge descent and re-ascension in which God dredged the salt and oozy bottom of Creation."

Here are the heights and depths for further study, but, again, we must try to define our terms. At the start of his book, C. S. Lewis writes:

"I use the word *Miracle* to mean an interference with Nature, by *super*natural power. This definition is not that which would be given by many theologians. I am adopting it, not because I think it an improvement upon theirs, but precisely because, being crude and 'popular' it enables me most easily to treat those questions which 'the common reader' probably has in mind when he takes up a book on Miracles."

Here then is a rough and ready definition of miracles, but the Church claims that miracles are not capricious, but are as much part of God's will and purpose and action as the miracle of Creation, which set our Universe in motion, and provides the continuing dependable laws of Nature, which maintains the life on earth of sceptic and believer alike.

Sceptical theologians take a fundamentalist view that God *cannot* change the course of natural laws; that he *ought not* to do so, if he is true to his impartial nature; and that in the birth and Resurrection of Jesus, he *did not* change the observed patterns of the laws of nature, as they understand scientific but sceptical scholars to perceive them, in their day. I say "in their day", because the intellectual arguments following the observable discovery of laws of nature a hundred or so years ago have gradually abated, as positive and theological scholars, with reverence for the authority and revelation of the Scriptures, have also come to understand natural law, and learnt to harmonise the natural and the supernatural, in our day. Today's sceptics suggest that early Christians did not know the laws of nature, but that now they do know them, logically God cannot change those laws. The sceptics say, "The early Christians believed that Jesus was conceived by the Holy Ghost, and born of the Virgin Mary, because, of course, they simply didn't know the laws of nature in the first century of Jesus' birth. Now we do have scientific knowledge, we believe that such a so-called 'miracle' should not, perhaps ought not, indeed *did* not, take place."

But this is absurd, if we take the story of Joseph, as described earlier in this book, at its face value, concerning his relations with the Virgin Mary. When Joseph discovered that Mary, to whom at this time he was only engaged, was pregnant, not unnaturally he decided to repudiate her as quietly and honourably as possible, for "he was a just man" (Matthew 1:19), and did not wish to hurt or humiliate her. His action was a sad but proper reaction to the observable fact of a pre-marital pregnancy. Why should he plan to do this? He knew, just as well as any modern gynaecologist, that in the ordinary course of nature, young women do *not* have babies unless they have had intercourse with men. No doubt modern gynaecologists and obstetricians know a variety of truths about birth and about begetting babies which Joseph in a so-called "pre-scientific age" did not know, but they do not alter the main thrust of this argument. A virgin birth is contrary to the course of nature. Joseph knew *that*. When Joseph accepted the fact that Mary was pregnant, not due to unchastity, but to a miracle (or even a "sign" as suggested in Matthew 1:23 and Isaiah 7:14), he accepted that the miracle or sign was something contrary to the known order of nature. All records of miracles teach this, and if we believe that God did not stop working miracles at Creation, it is surely logically congruous to believe that God can, and should, and indeed in probability *would*, use signs and miracles to usher in the New Creation in his Son?

We used C. S. Lewis's rough definition that the word "miracle" means an interference with Nature by supernatural power, but C. S. Lewis in his book *Miracles*, from which I have gratefully drawn in this chapter, is too shrewd a logical and theological scholar to stop there. Miracles done by God evoke wonder, and excite awe, or religious fear, and draw our attention to unique acts of God, which go beyond and above his natural laws.

For some months, when bishop's duties have taken me into the House of Lords at Westminster, I have heard the chimes of Big Ben, but the face of the great clock beneath the bell has been shrouded in scaffolding and opaque sheeting. Yet the chimes of Big Ben kept reminding me that I would soon see again that miracle of accurate time-keeping on the four faces of the clock. The preparatory chimes are a parable to me of the first miracle of the Messiah, who by the Virginal Conception was about to break into his world nine months later, as not only "Son of Mary", sharing our common humanity, but as "Son of God", revealing his divine nature, incarnate in human form.

The author of John's Gospel, that "beloved disciple" who was so close to his master, takes up this theme in the homely and joyful story of the village wedding at Cana of Galilee (John 2:1–11). The mother of Jesus, remembering perhaps the painful shock of her pregnancy, and nine months later the joyful wonder of his birth, says to the servants at a point of near catastrophe for the unnamed young bridal couple, "Whatever He says to you, do it." Quietly and authoritatively, Jesus issues his commands, and the miracle of turning water into wine occurs. There are no half-measures. There is enough for all, and "you have kept the *good* wine until now," says the puzzled steward of the feast to the bridegroom. It was a quietly unobtrusive, but kindly miracle, known to the servants of the bridegroom and the disciples, but not to the steward or, probably, the other wedding guests. It had deep significance, however, for the early members of the future apostolic band. John records:

"This, the first of his miracles (Authorised Version) or signs (Revised Standard Version), Jesus did at Cana in Galilee, and manifested his glory, and his disciples believed in Him."

To continue the Houses of Parliament picture, the chimes of Big Ben represented the call to recognise the miracle of his birth. The steady striking of the hours represent Christ's own miracles during his ministry, which John draws attention to, whereas the three Synoptic

Gospel writers simply record Christ's miracles. Matthew refers to Old Testament prophecies, but generally they report the miracles with a naturalness of writing, which implies that if Jesus is born in a miraculous way (Matt. 1:18–25 and Luke 1:25–56, 2:1–20) it is to be expected that he would in turn do miracles of gracious healing, and even subdue natural forces.

Although, as we have seen, John's Gospel speaks of miracles as signs of the Kingdom, which both promote faith and glorify God, Jesus often told his inner circle *not* to proclaim the fact of miracles, "until after he had risen from the dead" (Mark 9:1–10). See, here, the story of the Transfiguration, and the great miracle on the mountain top when his glory was revealed to Peter, James and John, and they heard the voice of the Father, saying "This is my beloved Son: listen to him" (v. 7).

The faith of the Church is inseparable from faith in the miracles of Christ's birth, Christ's serving ministry, his redemptive death, and his victorious Resurrection. There is a wholeness and a cohesion about the revelation of the Bible, the declaration of the Creeds, the proclamation of faith by every deacon and priest and bishop of the Church of England at his ordination and consecration, and the testimony of millions of believing Christians down the centuries. This cohesion of faith is tragically torn, if a significant body of senior churchmen unites to deny the miraculous content of our unique and historic Christian Faith.

Douglas Webster, former Canon of St. Paul's Cathedral and travelling theologian of the Church Missionary Society, referring to the summary of the Easter miracle in 1 Corinthians 15:3–4, once said: "Our Christian faith is built upon an event-theology, and not only on an idea-theology." Christ's saving death for our sins, and his miraculous rising from the dead "on the third day" (v. 4) are rooted in a time-space continuum. The Cross was rammed down into real earth on the hill of Calvary at Passover-time, when the city of Jerusalem was crowded, and thousands saw it and its victim, even though they may not have understood his atoning work. A real and heavy stone was removed from the door of the tomb, so that not only the startled disciples, but the silenced enemies, saw the tomb was empty, and discovered the body of Jesus was not there. The hearers at Peter's Pentecost Sermons may not have understood the miracle which Peter proclaimed, that "God raised this Jesus from the dead," but they were in no doubt that the body of Jesus was no longer in the empty tomb.

The chief priests and the Pharisees may have been increasingly opposed to Jesus, and his quiet claims to be the Christ, but they could not deny the sheer miracle of the raising of Lazarus from death after four days: "What shall we do? For this man performs many signs ("miracles" Authorised Version). If we let him go on thus, everyone will believe in him, and the Romans will come and destroy both our holy place and our nation" (John 11:47–48). ". . . so from that day on, they took counsel how to put Jesus to death" (v. 53). Paradoxically, it was the very miracle of Lazarus' resuscitation which finally persuaded the opposition to put Jesus to death. This in turn led to the great miracle, not only of Jesus being like Lazarus resuscitated, but being raised to newness of life in his resurrection body. His body was alike, but transformed, recognisable to the eye of faith, for Jesus was the same personality they had always known, but gloriously changed. "He was the first fruit of them that slept" (1 Cor. 15:20). Because of this unique and central miracle of Christ Jesus being raised from the dead "on the third day" we are assured by Paul that "we all shall be changed" and we have the promise of a like resurrection body in heaven one day. But without miracle, we are without hope, for "if Christ has not been raised, then our preaching is in vain, and your faith is in vain" (v. 14). "We are even found to be misrepresenting God, because we testified of God that he raised Christ, whom he did not raise, if it is true that the dead are not raised" (v. 15). Paul continues his logical progression: "If the dead are not raised, then Christ has not been raised. If Christ has not been raised, your faith is futile, and you are still in your sins" (v. 16–17). Paul goes even further in his clear argument: "Then those also who have fallen asleep in Christ have perished. If in this life *only* we have hoped in Christ, we are of all men most to be pitied" (v. 18–19).

Here Paul reaches the very nadir of religion without miracle, without hope, and so without a miraculous Gospel to offer with joy to a dying world. Paul then speaks with dramatic contrast.

"But, in fact, Christ has been raised from the dead, the first fruits of those who have fallen asleep. For as by man came death, by a man has come also the resurrection from the dead" (vv. 20, 21).

This cosmic nature of the death of Jesus is movingly described by C. S. Lewis in his chapter, "The Grand Miracle".

"But only a Man who did not need to have been a Man at all, unless He had chosen, only one who served in our sad regiment as a volunteer, yet also one who was perfectly a man, could perform this perfect dying; and thus (which way you put it is unimportant) either defeat death, or redeem it. He tasted death on behalf of all others. He is the representative 'Die-er' of the Universe: and for that very reason, the Resurrection and the Life."

Here is miracle on the grand scale. But, sadly, in the Church of England today, we face division at this very central theme of the historic Faith. The present Archbishop of York is reported in *The Times* as saying that he has "an open mind" about miracles. But miracle is an essential ingredient of the Faith, so we should have, surely, an accepting mind about miracle, and especially if one is called to be a bishop or guardian of the Faith.

In our lengthy public debate in the February session of the General Synod of the Church in 1985, the Archbishop of York appeared to defend his consecration of Dr. David Jenkins in July 1984 in York Minster, when he spoke of "a hierarchy of faith", in reference to belief in the miracle of the Virgin Birth. Dr. David Jenkins, writing in his diocesan news letter for Easter 1985, to which I have already referred, spoke of not "pretending beliefs which one does not find sufficient reason for holding. In any case, the Empty Tomb cannot prove, does not establish, and may not even mean the Resurrection. See especially Matthew 28:11–15." Bishop Jenkins then says, "The alternative *rational* and *plausible* explanation that the disciples stole the body was around pretty early on." This choice from the wealth of the Easter narratives of the four Gospels is strange indeed. In the next paragraph I quote Matthew 28:11–15 in full, because it comes directly after the plain statements of vv. 1–10, when (v. 6) the angel at the open and empty tomb, from which (v. 2) the great stone had been rolled back, said to the women, "Do not be afraid; for I know that you seek Jesus who was crucified. He is not here: for he has risen, *as he said.* Come see the place where he (the Lord: margin) lay. Then go quickly, and tell his disciples that he has risen from the dead" (v. 5–7a). The angel then told them to go to Galilee, where faith beside the sea-side three long years before all began, and where by the sea and in the hills Jesus taught them. The emphasis on the unhurried meetings by Galilee is found in Matthew, in Mark, with the touching reference: "tell *Peter*" (Mark 16:7), who had so tragically denied the very Name of Jesus (John 21:1–23). Galilee was soon to become the training ground during the great forty days between "the third day" when he rose from the dead, and the day of Ascension when he returned to his Father's Glory. Meanwhile (Matt. 28:9–10) the first appearance of Jesus early on Easter Day took place: "So the women departed quickly from the tomb with fear and great joy, and ran to tell the disciples, and behold Jesus met them, and said 'Hail', and they came up and took hold of his feet and worshipped him. Then Jesus said to them, 'Do not be afraid: go and tell my brethren to go to Galilee, and there they will see me.'" Note that the angel only says "disciples" (v. 7), while Jesus generously calls the scattered flock "brethren".

How can it be that Dr. David Jenkins appears unconvinced by the plain and rough-hewn words, with hardly an adjective or a superlative, which tell the unvarnished truth of the miracle of the Resurrection of Jesus from the open and empty tomb on the first Easter Day, unless he cannot believe in the very principle of miracle, or of God's direct intervention in history, from Christ's birth, to death and renewed life on Easter Day? To pass over Matthew 28:1–10, and then to turn our thoughts to vv. 11 to 15 alone seems the very weakest sort of "fundamentalism", which elsewhere he abhors. "Fundamentalism", in its pejorative sense, is to take a verse or verses out of context, to lay the weight of a general doctrine upon one particular text, and not to compare text with text, and Biblical passage with other Biblical passages, to discover the main tenor of truth, which in this case refers to the historical fact which Peter proclaimed in the first Pentecost, and post-Resurrection sermon:

"Men of Israel, hear these words: Jesus of Nazareth, a man attested to you by God with mighty works and wonders and signs which God did through him in your midst, as you yourselves know – this Jesus, delivered up according to the definite plan and foreknowledge of God, you crucified and killed by the hands of lawless men. But God raised him up, having loosed the pangs of death, because it was not possible for him to be held by it. For David says concerning him, 'I saw the Lord always before me, for he is at my right hand that I may not be shaken; therefore my heart was glad, and my tongue rejoiced; moreover my flesh will dwell in hope. For thou wilt not abandon my soul to Hades, nor let thy Holy One see corruption. Thou has made known to me the ways of life; thou wilt make me full of gladness with thy presence'" (Acts 2:22–28). See also Acts 2:29–36, Acts 3:12–21, Acts 4:1–4, Acts 4:8–12.

Within the lengthy, historic, and unrefuted preaching of Peter, the young apostle, concerning Christ's Resurrection, "and of that we all are witnesses" (2:33), Dr. Jenkins takes these next verses to which he turns our thoughts, which he puts forward as "the alternative rational and plausible explanation, that the disciples stole the body", and he adds this story "was around pretty soon".

"While (the women) were going, behold, some of the guard went into the city and told the chief priests all that had taken place. And when they had assembled with the elders and taken counsel, they gave a sum of money to the soldiers and said, 'Tell people, "His disciples came by night and stole him away while we were asleep." And if this comes to the governor's ears, we will satisfy him and keep you out of trouble.' So they took the money and did as they were directed; and this story has been spread among the Jews to this day" (Matt. 28:11–15).

But what does Dr. Jenkins *mean*? Does he believe these verses (11–15) but not the earlier ones (1–10)? Does he believe the lies of the chief priests and the elders that the body of Jesus was stolen in the night? Does he believe that the leaders bribed the soldiers to spread this dreadful lie abroad? Does he believe the record of Matthew that "this story has been spread among the Jews to this day" (v. 15)? How much does he feel able to pick and choose as truth, and reject as error, in all the 15 verses of Matthew 28:1–15? Is he really offering the lies of the opposition, rather than the witness of the women, and later of the disciples, as the Christian Gospel which as a bishop he is consecrated to proclaim, and commissioned to guard?

Professor Sir Norman Anderson, formerly Chairman of the House of Laity of the General Synod, in *The Evidence for the Resurrection* (I.V.P.) argues cogently for the historic case for belief in Christ's bodily resurrection, and in studying the objections, in this case, states:

"Is it conceivable that a deliberate lie would change a company of cowards into heroes, and inspire them to a life of sacrifice, often ending only in martyrdom? Surely psychology teaches that nothing makes a man more prone to cowardice than a lie which preys upon his conscience? Is it likely, moreover, that even in disillusionment or agony not a single one of these conspirators would ever have divulged the secret?" The pages of history are silent about such a deception, but the lips of all the early Christians maintain the testimony of Romans 10:9, 'If you confess with your lips that Jesus is LORD, and believe in your heart that God raised Him from the dead, you will be saved.'"

When "the priests and captains of the Temple and the Sadducees came upon Peter and John, and were annoyed because they were teaching the people and proclaiming their belief in 'Jesus and the resurrection from the dead'" (Acts 4:1–4) why did they not boldly accuse them of stealing the dead body? Why did they not produce the body themselves, knowing their lies had no foundation? They were silent, in Jerusalem itself.

The early chapters of Acts demonstrate that though the young disciples may have been "uneducated and common men" (Acts 4:13), they not only worked miracles in the Saving Name of the risen Jesus (Acts 3:14–16), but they boldly witnessed immediately that though "you killed the Author of life, whom God raised from the dead", the disciples could say, "To this we are witnesses", and "many of those who heard the word believed, and the number of the men came to about five thousand" (Acts 4:4).

Dr. Jenkins mentions "the alternative rational and plausible explanation that the disciples stole the body (which) was around pretty early on". But this is to cast chilling doubts on the veracity and so the integrity of the apostolic witnesses. This is to deny the early chapters of Church history, joyfully and strenuously set out in Acts 1–5. Above and beyond all, this is to question not only the full record of Scripture concerning the events of Easter Day, plainly set out, and built into the Creeds of the Church. This is to question the procession of miracles from the Virginal Conception to the great Resurrection miracle, that God had broken into our world, spoiled by sin, to redeem mankind by miracles of supernature in the Person of his Son.

I want to be as fair as I can to Bishop Jenkins, but if he stands by his "alternative and plausible explanation that the disciples stole the body . . ." then Peter is a liar when he publicly stated "This Jesus God raised up, and of that we all are witnesses" (Acts 2:32). He is in conspiracy with "the disciples (who) stole the body". The early and cohesive apostolic witness to the historical events of Easter Day was built on corporate falsehood. Jesus constantly spoke of being "the Truth" (John 14:6), and clearly and often taught that "on the third day, he would rise again" (Mark 10:34). All Jerusalem knew this claim, and cast it in his teeth, even as he hung upon the Cross, with bitter cruelty: "And those who passed by derided Jesus, wagging their heads, and saying 'Aha! You who would destroy the Temple and build it *in three days*, save yourself, and come down from the cross'" (Mark 15:29–30).

Philosophically, can we believe that the God of truth, whose Son came, both to save us, and to lead us into all truth, would have accepted the flawed, deceptive, and dishonest witness of the early disciples?

This, surely, is the logical progression of casting doubt on the events of Easter Day. No one can be made to believe, but if we believe, we are called to believe in an historic faith which is inseparable from miracle. As bishops we are called to lead people from rational doubting to equally rational faith, for the very word "disciple" speaks of a learner.

I recognise that in this chapter, and earlier in this book, I have been critical of a fellow-bishop, but because news travels so fast today, and the Good News of the many bishops who hold the Biblical and Catholic faith of the Church of England in its fulness is seldom made public, I believe it is right to speak out on an issue which affects the health of the Church. Sadly, I still see and hear no clear evidence that makes me withdraw my public statement that if Dr. David Jenkins, whom I like as a person, continues to teach a defective faith, he should give prolonged and serious thought about resigning the teaching and pastoring office of a diocesan bishop. Our responsibilities, as bishops, to guard and teach the historic catholic faith of the Church, are very weighty. Our opportunities joyfully and confidently to proclaim the Gospel of Christ as Redeemer and Risen Lord are very great. Our commission at our consecration to state that we believe the authority of the Bible, and teach it in its fulness, calls on us to be "ready, with all faithful diligence, to banish and drive away all erroneous and strange doctrine contrary to God's Word; and both privately and openly to call upon and encourage others to do the same?" (One of the archbishop's questions in the Prayer Book Service for the Consecration of Bishops.)

My case rests here. But let me finish this chapter by opening up the theme of the next chapter. Miracles did not end with the Ascension, because every time an unbeliever is led to a vivid faith in the Christian Gospel, and a surly rebel against God turns in repentance to an obedient faith in Jesus Christ as living Saviour, and openly proclaims that "Jesus is Lord", the individual miracle of the new birth, or regeneration, takes place in the individual soul. These miracles recur, day by day, wherever the Gospel is preached throughout the world.

I intend to illustrate from living examples, in the next chapter, what the miracle of the new birth means today. I quote extensively from C. S. Lewis's own testimony of his Christian conversion. Statistically, most people come to faith in Christ by their late teens, but I am writing a book for all ages. For the first time, in 1984, in our diocese of Norwich, in twos and threes and usually in family groups, over 500 of our Confirmation candidates were over twenty-one years of age. A few were in their sixties and seventies, and as each congregation called out boldly, using the title of this book – "This is *our* Faith" – whole families, sometimes three generations, professed their faith in Christ.

Yet it is easy to believe that if one has not experienced a living meeting with Jesus Christ in one's teens, it is too late to meet vividly with Christ in one's forties. I print C. S. Lewis's "testimony" in full as a preparation for the next chapter.

Men are reluctant to pass over from the notion of an abstract and negative deity to the living God. I do not wonder. Here lies the deepest tap-root of Pantheism and of the objection to traditional imagery. It was hated not, at bottom, because it pictured Him as man but because it pictured Him as king, or even as warrior. The Pantheist's God does nothing, demands nothing. He is there if you wish for Him, like a book on a shelf. He will not pursue you. There is no danger that at any time heaven and earth should flee away at His glance. If He were the truth, then we could really say that all the Christian images of kingship were a historical accident of which our religion ought to be cleansed. It is with a shock that we discover them to be indispensable. You have had a shock like that before, in connection with smaller matters – when the line pulls at your hand, when something breathes beside you in the darkness. So here; the shock comes at the precise moment when the thrill of *life* is communicated to us along the clue we have been following. It is always shocking to meet life where we thought we were alone. "Look out!" we cry, "It's *alive*." And therefore this is the very point at which so many draw back – I would have done so myself if I could – and proceed no further with Christianity. An "impersonal" God – well and good. A subjective God of beauty, truth and goodness, inside our own heads – better still. A formless life-force surging through us, a vast power which we can tap – best of all. But God Himself, alive, pulling at the other end of the cord, perhaps approaching at an infinite speed, the hunter, king, husband – that is quite another matter. There comes a moment when the children who have been playing at burglars hush suddenly: was that a *real* foot-step in the hall? There comes a moment when people who have been dabbling in religion ("Man's search for God!") suddenly draw back. Supposing we really found Him? We never meant it to come to *that*! Worse still, supposing He had found us? So it is a sort of Rubicon. One goes across; or not. But if one does, there is no manner of security against miracles. One may be in for *anything*.

12

A PRACTICAL FAITH FOR TODAY

I remember a David Langton cartoon in *Punch* depicting an elderly and scholarly clergyman leaning over his pulpit and saying to his sparse but startled congregation: "I know what you will say to me – Sabellianism."

You may feel that the previous chapter on miracles is somewhat esoteric for straightforward practical Christian laymen.

I believe that the assurance of the historic, unique, and miraculous events which surround the earthly life and work of Jesus are in fact the solid ground on which we can be assured of a practical faith that works today and changes our lives.

In this chapter, therefore, I want to paint a gallery of mainly unnamed but representative portraits, who to my certain knowledge have found the resting place of their faith in the living Christ, and have then gone forward "in his service, which is perfect freedom", as the Prayer Book collect puts it. I will change some Christian names, but they are real people whom I know personally, not just representative figures to illustrate a point. I write of them, trusting that their story may chime in with your situation, because the state of our world today calls for resolute Christians, with such a clear and positive faith, that self-forgetfully they can share that faith with others.

I shall range backwards and forwards across the forty-five years of my ministry, because I want sometimes to speak of men and women whose faith has stood the test of time, and is still bright and reproductive in the lives of others today.

On D-Day I discovered that the senior doctor of the beachhead where I landed that day, on the left of the British and Canadian assault, was a convinced and practising Christian. As doctors and chaplains we carry no weapons, of course, but are wholly at the service of our wounded and dying men. Dr. Paul, already decorated with the Military Cross for gallantry during the withdrawal of Dunkirk in 1940, received an immediate Bar to his M.C. for his courage, and compassion amongst the wounded, in the four busy weeks after D-Day, before our beach which was under constant shellfire and air-attack was closed, when the Mulberry Harbour further to the west was operating well.

Dr. Paul's faith steadied us all, and when a young corporal called Charlie was severely wounded in the spine, he advised me to go, with him, to the Field Dressing Station near Douvre la Deliverande, telling me he probably only had three or four days to live. We read John 14:1–6, in the time-honoured Authorised Version, as the ambulance bumped along the shell-marked beach lateral road.

"Jesus said: 'Let not your heart be troubled: ye believe in God, believe also in me. In my Father's house are many mansions: if it were not so, I would have told you. I go to prepare a place for you. And if I go and prepare a place for you, I will come again, and receive you unto myself; that where I am, there ye may be also. And whither I go ye know, and the way ye know.' Thomas said unto him, 'Lord, we know not whither thou goest; and how can we know the way?' Jesus saith unto him, 'I am the way, the truth, and the life: no man cometh unto the Father, but by me.'"

I had come straight to the chaplaincy service of the Royal Navy, from three years in London, during the London "Blitz", under a great and godly vicar, Prebendary Colin Kerr, who had been an Army chaplain in World War I and had told me how in that war, in which I myself had been born, he used to say to his soldiers in danger or when wounded: "It's trusting Jesus and trusting him all the way," based on these great promises of Christ in St. John's Gospel.

In the three days that young Charlie's physical life was ebbing away, I watched his Christian faith steadily growing as he would say with me: "It's trusting Jesus, and trusting him all the way", and as he read as best he could from the small "Active Service" New Testament I had given him. "I've been saying my prayers today, Padre," Charlie said to me with a smile, on my last visit to him before he died on the Sunday, twelve days after D-Day. The French children came and reverently placed June roses on his simple grave. I have never forgotten, because I saw the quiet individual miracle of re-generation, or new birth, taking place before my eyes, as Charlie had three conscious days quietly to make his peace with God.

A harrowing story? No, not for his mother and his girl-friend in South London, when some weeks later, between postings in Normandy, I was able to visit them, and other bereaved relatives, and also the wounded back in the hospitals of England. Charlie had died in faith. I had been strengthened in my own belief in the power of re-generation, or "being born again, or anew, or from above" as Jesus vividly put it to Nicodemus (John 3:1–8).

But it was the quality of faith of Dr. Paul, with time to care personally for each wounded man, that made its impact on me.

I realised that nothing was so important as caring for the individual, and that a committed Christian takes a balanced view of men's need for salvation through faith in Christ, as well as their need for physical and mental health.

When I was recently preaching in Hong Kong, forty years on from D-Day, I met up with Dr. Paul again, in the medical missionary hospital where for very many years he had been medical superintendent. Despite a stroke, which had impaired his speech, his faith in Christ was as strong as ever. When we find Christ as our own Friend and

Saviour when we are young students, we have the privilege of a whole lifetime of useful service for others, for his sake. In Hong Kong, Dr. Paul introduced me to a young Chinese student, very severely paralysed in a wheelchair, following a major accident four years earlier.

The student had no Christian faith at the time of the accident, and was nearly totally incapacitated. His mind was clear, however, and painfully he got fellow students round him to sign a petition to the Governor to allow him to be subjected to "euthanasia", the inaccurately called "mercy-killing", because he felt life had no meaning. Dr. Paul told me how the young student had been slowly and patiently led to put his trust and faith in Jesus Christ. When Dr. Paul introduced me, and I held the Chinese student's hand in mine, slowly and haltingly doctor and patient together spoke of Christ, and how the student had been now able to gather a few other Chinese students around his wheelchair for Bible-reading as he shared his new-found faith with them. There is an enduring quality about a true faith in Christ, which is self-authenticating, and leads to unselfish service.

James came out of the Army, and was a member of our congregation at St. Ebbe's, Oxford, where he was a post-war undergraduate. In place of a car he owned an old second-hand hearse with Victorian-type tasselled blinds on the windows. James with John, a former naval submariner, and with a former W.A.A.F. and a young undergraduate called Tony, whose parents were very opposed to his new-found Christianity, were very keen to put their faith into action. They travelled up the hill in the hearse to one of the hospitals in Oxford where there was a children's ward, and asked the Ward Sister if they could run a Sunday School for her children. Sister agreed, calling James and John her "Apostles", and the Sunday School started. Mary, the Staff Nurse, was so intrigued by these cheerful ex-service officers, who appeared to have a practical faith in Christ, which spurred them into action, that she offered to help in the Sunday School, and joined the hearse party to St. Ebbe's Church. Mary had been educated at a good Anglo-Catholic girls school, staffed by Anglican nuns who cared for her deeply. Her father was a country clergyman, of a second or third generation parson family. She was a fairly typical, honest, sincere Church of England girl, trained to high standards in one of the great London teaching hospitals. She discovered that though she held to the basic doctrines of the Church she neither had the strong desire to teach others about Jesus Christ as her new-found Oxford friends clearly did, nor the assurance of a personal knowledge of Christ which gave her such a desire.

"For too long," she said, "I have been trying to get to God, but I have been by-passing Jesus Christ." She began to understand what Jesus meant, when he said "I am the Way, the Truth, and the Life: no man comes to the Father but by me" (John 14:6). The witness of her friends, the understanding that Christ is the Mediator without whom we cannot reach God, the sincerity to search with all her heart until she found Christ, and the regular teaching from the Bible of her local parish church, gradually led her to the place of personal commitment in obedience to Christ as Saviour and Lord. As a professional and efficient staff nurse, she had found before her conversion that she did not know what to say to dying patients. When she came to know Christ for herself she discovered she could share her faith in Christ who in his Resurrection had conquered death. It was a very practical result for her, which stood her in good stead when later she became a Ward Sister. Later, Christian marriage, the birth of children, one to become a nurse, and another an ordinand, with opportunities of Christian service and especially in hospice work, all stemmed from the infection of faith, caught from those young contemporaries in Oxford.

But the Christian Faith is not synonymous with culture and Oxbridge privileges, even though Oxford and Cambridge have in these post-war years been seedbeds of faith, where, in addition to the strenuous work of college chaplains, half a dozen churches have produced a steady and enthusiastic stream of ordination candidates of high calibre, whose influence is now increasingly felt in the ministry of the Church.

A personal faith is by no means synonymous with a call to ordained service, although, in fact, James of the hearse was ordained, and later became a Service chaplain, but not before he had led a fellow Oxford student, Thomas, to faith in Christ. After a number of years as a parish clergyman Thomas became the Principal of a Theological College, and as a scholarly disciplined, pastorally-minded principal, has been exercising a powerful influence in the Church through the Ordinands committed to his charge and care.

Sometimes sincere church-goers are nervous of moving forward from safe and rather passive church membership into areas of "personal conversion" or "commitment to Christ", for which they may feel that "enthusiasm is a very horrid thing." My memory of this period is more of seriousness, than emotion however.

Jock had been a "gunner" officer in Italy, and was once on top of a hill in a forward observation post for his battery, when he discovered the Germans were ranging on him: a hundred yards behind, fifty yards ahead, and Jock was stung into prayer. He was a clever young man, with a place already offered to him at Oxford. "O God, if there be a God," the cautious young Scot began, "If you will get me out of this alive, when I get to Oxford I will search for you until I find you." He returned alive and found Bishop Stephen Neill conducting an evangelistic mission in Oxford, which by the bishop's combination of evangelistic clarity, deep Biblical scholarship and a very human approachability, had a powerful impact on many lives. Jock, after graduation, became a don in Cambridge, and as a layman in College, and a lay reader in his local church, exercised a long and useful ministry. He has recently been ordained as a non-stipendiary minister in the Church of England, after retiring from his scientific academic work. His practical faith stemmed from a serious and whole-hearted committal of the will to God in Christ, for whom he searched determinedly.

147

Another student had served in the Brigade of Guards, and one Sunday morning at St. Ebbe's Church, in place of the sermon, I invited, with the bishop's permission (I seem to remember being a law-abiding young rector at the time!), four students to speak for exactly five minutes each, to testify to their new-found faith. A working faith grows and deepens when we let it be known we are on the side of Christ, and I believe we have to break through the "sound barrier" of silence, as Christians, and share our faith with others, as I found the Ugandan Christians do so bravely, when last I was in that beautiful but sometimes dangerous country, where the Church is so courageous.

Martin's sermon was short and to the point. In summary, he said, "As I had served in the Brigade of Guards (and he named his regiment), when I first began to understand, and to search for, a faith that works, I saw it in military terms. Who gives the final orders in my life? Christ, or myself, and I saw it must be Christ." As he grew in faith and grace from that personal committal to Christ, I coveted him for ordained service. At a student conference, I put this to him. He listened with care and courtesy. "No, Maurice," he said, "I'm quite sure that God wants me in politics." I was surprised, because in those days the Church was slow to see the need of really committed Christians in Parliament, in the Civil Service, in the Press and in so-called "secular" pursuits. We were wrong, and the situation is much better today. In the ten years I have been on the Bishops' Bench in the House of Lords, it has become a very natural thing amongst many Anglican and Roman Catholic Christian friends in the House, to promise prayer support for one another, not only in sickness or bereavement, but before someone who shares faith with you, of whatever party, is due to make a difficult speech and especially a Maiden Speech. Naturally most temporal peers, who are not crossbenchers, owe firm allegiance to one or other of the great political parties. Almost without exception, however, bishops try to speak "in the national interest" and not in terms of "party politics", but so many matters for debate are non-party-political but are ethical or social or medical, that committed Christians find themselves very properly taking council together.

In recent years debates on educational matters, on the revision of the Mental Health Act, on divorce matters and the control of ideas on the Warnock Report on embryology; on race relations and the protection of the Christian insights brought with clarity and conviction by peers of all parties and denominations, who share strong Christian convictions concerning faith in Christ, and the outworking of that faith, in daily life. I must pay tribute to the work of the Order of Christian Unity with its various specialised sub-committees and the work of CARE campaigns under Raymond Johnston's energetic leadership and the briefs to us bishops from the General Synod boards, that help us come to informed judgments on complicated and sometimes contentious issues.

But the Palace of Westminster is, outside the debates, not unlike a very large and busy village. As a fairly regular attender when diocesan duties allow it, I have found myself, as other bishops on the Bench also find, that we are often seen as a "village vicar", more than as a distant prelate. I count as my honoured friends our doorkeepers (all of whom are former senior N.C.O.s of the three Services), the policemen and policewomen, the secretaries and officers of the House, the security guards and the cleaning ladies, the men and women in our restaurant and in the canteen, and the host of others. They have shared their faith, or aired their doubts. We have talked of Christ as living Lord in practical terms. I have tried to share Christ's comfort and his triumph over death, with those who are sick or bereaved. Throughout these ten years in the House of Lords, I have realised there is residual faith in so many, but I have also experienced the need of speaking from quiet assurance about Christ as living Lord and Master for the clarifying of faith. Our Lord once said, "Let not your heart be troubled, you believe in God, believe also in me" (John 14:1). As clergy we are called to lead others to an ever deeper and clearer faith in Jesus Christ. We can only do this if down the years our own faith is deepening and maturing, as areas of residual doubt give place to new areas of experiencing God in Christ, as we continue daily to study the Bible, which is truly the Word of God.

Because I am writing this final chapter in the last year of my stipendiary whole-time ministry as Bishop of Norwich, I have been drawing encouragement from looking back on my past files and records and seeing where I happen by coincidence to be able to mark the maturing of faith, and its results in action today.

Conversions do not simply happen only on a one-to-one basis. I have found there are principles to be understood if evangelism is to be both continuous in its outreach, and lasting in its results.

Archbishop William Temple said: "The Gospel is true always and everywhere, or it is not a Gospel at all, or true at all." Because Jesus gave as his last post-Resurrection commission a universal command, we can believe this. "Go into all the world, and make disciples of *every* nation" (Matthew 28:19).

The best definition is that of the report "Towards the Conversion of England" (1945) taken from the Archbishop's Call to Evangelism in 1918 and quoted again in the 1970s by the recent Archbishop's Council for Evangelism, on which I served:

"To evangelise is to present Christ Jesus in the power of the Holy Spirit, that men shall come to put their trust in God through Him, to accept Him as their Saviour, and serve Him as their King in the fellowship of His Church."

Our Lord himself did this work by loving, by serving and by telling. I find today that when local churches in Baker Street or Oxford, in Islington or Kampala, in Norwich or in Norfolk villages, seriously consider how best they can evangelise, and then start doing it, people find Christ and are built into the fellowship of his Church.

Dr. Leighton Ford in his book *The Christian Persuaders: A new look at Evangelism today* isolates these three strands and presents them in their Biblical context. He speaks of the local church, and its opportunities of winning people to the faith of Christ by KOINONIA – the witness of fellowship; by DIAKONIA – the witness of service, and by KERYGMA – the witness of proclamation.

The present Archbishop of Canterbury followed his predecessor in this theme, by saying that unless a Christian activity was local it was not real.

Because I have spent so much of my ministry in parishes, I have a continuing confidence in the Church of England's ability to increase its immensely widespread evangelistic activity. When I read recently a report on "Dead Rural Anglicanism", I simply did not recognise the picture drawn by a research sociologist, compared with the vitality of the local churches I know all over Norfolk today.

Where the local church, however small, really shows these three marks of Christian fellowship, Christian service, and Christian proclamation of the evangel, the church grows. Certainly the day of the parish mission is returning, as I know from taking part in them regularly. Our Diocesan Missioner spent a whole year in preparing for one parish mission in a large commuter village outside Norwich. When I came to preach or speak each night, the parish was prepared by prayer, visiting, personal invitations, and contact with those recently married or confirmed or those who had brought their babies to baptism. There were long-term results, and in one year, I ordained three men from that parish, one stipendiary, and two non-stipendiary.

Family services, whether eucharistic or not, are proving evangelistic, and I seldom confirm without finding that a mother or father are being confirmed with one of their children. For the first time in 1984, over 500 of our candidates were over twenty-one years of age. Many were renewing their baptismal promises publicly and locally after making their commitment to Christ openly known at our Mission England meetings with Dr. Graham, last year.

When the vicar proclaims with confidence the Gospel of Christ, and offers personal counselling with trained counsellors, mainly already equipped in Mission England

Life and Witness Classes, and where preaching is under-girded with prayer, and parishioners bring their friends, people are converted in towns and villages. Often the mission work is ecumenical. Nothing takes the place of the Church of England doing its own duty to the nation, by presenting the Gospel clearly, lovingly and compellingly in the local parish situation.

In the second chapter of 1 Peter, this same strategy is unfolded as Peter calls us to Christ the Rock of Ages, who is precious to those who believe. Next he calls the living stones to be knit into a holy temple, to offer up spiritual worship. Then he calls the congregation to show forth the light of the Gospel, to a dark world outside. Our Lambeth Conference of 1978 summed up the strategy well when it said, "The Church gathers for worship and scatters for mission." It is a glorious thing in a confirmation, great or small, to call out boldly (in the title of this book), "This is our Faith", but the witness must then be taken to the world outside the confines of the building.

I finish this chapter with three illustrations, one from the Services, one from the Arts, and one from the world of literature, to encourage any who are still struggling through areas of doubt, or sorrow, or intellectual confusion, but who desire more fully to know Christ as "the Way, the Truth, and the Life" and are beginning to see that "no one comes to the Father, but by me" (John 14:6). For reasons that will appear, I use my friends' own names, and I call them to witness with me, to the sufficiency of Christ in widely differing circumstances. I humbly invite them to say with me, "This is our Faith".

I have before me a copy of *Practical Christianity*, the journal of the Officers' Christian Union for July/August 1956, nearly 30 years ago. I had been speaking at their annual meeting, having been deeply involved in O.C.U. matters as a naval chaplain myself.

The simple thought I bring you is that wherever we may be (and in the Services it does seem that some of you are always on the move) God is there. "Whither shall I go from Thy Spirit? Or whither shall I flee from Thy presence?" When I was flying out to India at 10,000 feet I read: "If I ascend up into heaven Thou art there" (v. 8), and wondered whether I was reading it higher up than anyone else had done! The Bible fits into our situation, whether in the excitement of active service or in the day-to-day living as Christians.

"If I take the wings of the morning and dwell in the uttermost parts of the sea: even there shall Thy hand lead me" (vv. 9,10). These verses fit the R.A.F. and the Navy and every part of Service life. "Even there" sums up all that we read in the earlier verses of this psalm. Christ Jesus can be with us always, in all places. The Bible teaches us that if we are committed to the Lord Jesus Christ there is no distant place to which we may be sent in which we may not have our Lord and Saviour all the time (Rev. 3:20). "If any man hear my voice and open the door, I will come in to him. . . ." That is how we first can set up our relationship with Him. Then, wherever He sends us, He will go with us. "Go ye . . . and, lo, I am with you alway, even unto the end of the world" (Matt. 28:20).

In our normal Christian life, Bible-reading, prayer, Holy Communion, worship, fellowship are all generally necessary to our spiritual health. These are ways in which God in His mercy feeds and strengthens us. But it is a wonderful thing to know that if through force of circumstances all these things are taken away from us, if we are committed to Christ we are His for ever and He is with us. A young man, who became an officer in the Merchant Navy after he had served in the Royal Navy during the war, had come to Christ when he was at school and served Him in Christian fellowship and different ways while in the Navy. After the war he served two years abroad in the Merchant Navy and did not meet another Christian with whom he could have fellowship or opportunity for Christian worship except occasionally when he went ashore in foreign waters. "But", he said, "I proved Christ with me". As a result of finding Christ's sufficiency when entirely alone, he is now training for full-time Christian service. God has to be trusted everywhere and there is no place where we may not know him and trust him. We may have his presence all the time. We should not despise the different meetings and means of grace that God gives to us, but we should not despair when we have not got them. Trust him and trust him fully. I know we are in so-called peacetime; but most of you who are younger are being rushed to various places of trouble in the world and are in dangers as in the war. Those of us who are in danger have the privilege of proving the reality of Christian testimony that he delivers from the fear of death. I do not mean the fear of being hurt or wounded, but the fear of death. If we are called to face death, we know we go to his immediate Presence.

I wrote those words nearly thirty years ago. Then I heard that that young Merchant Navy Officer had first gone out to East Africa, and then had been ordained, and later served for ten years in the Royal Army Chaplains' Department. He returned from the Army to do parish work in Suffolk. It was then a great joy to me to meet up with the Revd. John Howitt again, and Anne, his wife, and together they are now doing valuable work in three of our Norfolk parishes. John's faith in Christ has not only stood the test of time, but has helped him to bring others to faith in Christ in a steady, faithful way in rural Norfolk. So many village parishes are very much alive. I am finding that I totally reject the facile generalisation that Anglicanism is "dead" in rural areas. At a village wedding I was involved in yesterday the Team Vicar (3 clergy caring for 9 villages) said, "We have only thirty-seven people living in this tiny parish, but eighteen of them come to church." Another Team Rector and his wife responded to a request to read the Bible through in one of their churches. They began on Friday evening, and at 3.00 a.m. on Tuesday morning there were nearly twenty people in that other small village church as they completed a team of readers, in Revelation 22; I confirmed there recently. Village churches are alive in Norfolk.

Secondly, I look back only twenty years to our first meeting as a family with Martin Blogg, who was then a practical lecturer in dance and drama at the Trent Park Polytechnic (as it then was) to which one or two of our family went, after boarding school, to get "A" Levels "at deeper level" before University entrance. As a family (we have six children) we owed much to Martin's enthusiasm and expertise, and he often visited our home when I was Principal of Oak Hill Theological College. During this time Martin, a former member of the Royal Marines Band, came to put his trust and confidence in Christ, and because he regularly visits our home, he has become a tried and trusted friend. For this reason, my wife and I have been able to observe not only his growth in faith, but the way in which as a firmly believing Christian, God has developed his very special and unusual gifts of dance and its relation with worship. We have had groups of deeply committed young professionally trained ballet dancers doing workshops in schools in Norfolk, in our churches and in Norwich Cathedral. In the Preface to Martin Blogg's new book *Dance and the Christian Faith* (Hodder and Stoughton) I wrote of his pioneer spirit which came alive when he found faith in Christ. I said this:

Without peradventure, ever since Martin Blogg came to faith in Christ, and then began relating his faith to his profession of teaching Dance Drama he has steadily and persistently pioneered the task of relating the disciplines of a highly professional dancer to the study of the doctrines of the Christian faith (he has spent much time, studying at Oak Hill Theological College, with the encouragement of the former Principal, Canon David Wheaton).

Dance and the Christian Faith with its clear sections on 1. Dance and Scripture, 2. Dance and Education, 3. Religious Dance and its practical training, is a tribute to the work which Martin Blogg has pioneered in his own person. His non-verbal approach to Christian dance will open new avenues for the expression of the Faith, in parallel with the traditional ones of speech, liturgy and sacramental express.

Personal commitment to Christ releases energies in the soul that can transform us into workers for God, who can enthuse and equip others for Christian service.

Martin Blogg has the discipline and musicianship of the Royal Marines Band behind him with the professional training as a ballet dancer, and with the painstaking study of the Bible to understand Christian doctrine, as part of his burgeoning gifts to the Church. But it was personal commitment to Christ that galvanised him into this special pioneering work of relating dance and Christianity, and its use in worship, and so it must ever be, if the Church is to respond to the needs of the world. When the love of Christ grips our hearts at his Cross, we will be energised to take his love into the world, for which Christ died. The Church has many allies, when we are meeting the human needs of hunger, sickness and natural disasters, in the world. The Church has no ally, when it is engaged in its primary task of the salvation of eternal souls. If we fail here, we fail utterly. For their sake and for Christ's sake, we must *not* fail.

Finally, having written fully about C. S. Lewis in the chapter on miracles I call Sheldon Vanauken, author of the bestseller on both sides of the Atlantic, *A Severe Mercy*, to share his witness for Christ.

Sheldon Vanauken came as a research student to Oxford, after serving in the U.S. Navy and University work in America. Because he and "Davy" his wife came often to St. Ebbe's Church in Oxford, I got to know him well, and recognise his quality, his honest seeking for God and his sensitive humanity. The unpublished letters from C. S. Lewis to Sheldon are printed in this book, which helped him to faith. His doubts were so real, his hesitations so honest, but his search so brave, that I print the crisis of his conversion here (with permission).

C. S. Lewis, remembering perhaps his own intellectual, moral and emotional conversion to Christ, wrote to Sheldon: "But I think you are already in the meshes of the net! The Holy Spirit is after you. I doubt if you'll get away! Yours C. S. Lewis."

Sheldon writes:

This was getting serious. Alarm bells sounded, but I couldn't decide where to run.

Christianity now appeared intellectually stimulating and aesthetically exciting. The personality of Jesus emerged from the Gospels with astonishing consistency. Whenever they were written, they were written in the shadow of a personality so tremendous that Christians who may never have seen him knew him utterly: that strange mixture of unbearable sternness and heartbreaking tenderness. No longer did the Church appear only a disreputable congerie of quarrelling sects: now we saw the Church, splendid and terrible, sweeping down the centuries with anthems and shining crosses and steady-eyed saints. No longer was the Faith something for children: intelligent people held it strongly – and they walked to a secret singing that we could not hear. Or did we hear something: high and clear and unbearably sweet?

I wrote in my Journal:

It would seem that Christianity requires both emotional and intellectual assent. If there is only emotion, the mind asks troubling questions that, if not answered, might lead to a falling away, for love cannot be sustained without understanding. On the other hand, there is a gap which must be bridged by emotion. If one is suspicious of the upsurge of feeling that may be incipient faith, how is one to cross the gap?

Christianity – in a word, the divinity of Jesus – seemed probable to me. But there is a gap between the probable and proved. How was I to cross it? If I were to stake my whole life on the Risen Christ, I wanted proof. I wanted certainty. I wanted to see Him eat a bit of fish. I wanted

letters of fire across the sky. I got none of these. And I
continued to hang about on the edge of the gap.

Davy [his wife] and I, sometimes with friends, sometimes alone, were reading Dorothy Sayers's tremendous
series of short plays on the life of Jesus. In one of them,
I was forcibly struck by the reply of a man to Jesus's
inquiry about his faith: 'Lord, I believe; help thou mine
unbelief.' Wasn't that just my position? Believing and not
believing? A paradox, like that other paradox: one must
have faith to believe but must believe in order to have
faith. A paradox to unlock a paradox? I felt that it was.

One day later there came the second intellectual
breakthrough: it was the rather chilling realisation that *I
could not go back*. In my old easy-going theism, I had
regarded Christianity as a sort of fairy tale; and I had
neither accepted nor rejected Jesus, since I had never,
in fact, encountered him. Now I had. The position was
not, as I had been comfortably thinking all these
months, merely a question of whether I was to accept
the Messiah or not. It was a question of whether I was
to accept Him – or *reject*. My God! There was a gap
behind me, too. Perhaps the leap to acceptance was a
horrifying gamble – but what of the leap to rejection?
There might be no certainty that Christ was God – but,
by God, there was no certainty that He was not. If I
were to accept, I might and probably would face the
thought through the years: 'Perhaps, after all, it's a lie;
I've been had!' But if I were to reject, I would certainly
face the haunting, terrible thought: "Perhaps it's true –
and I have *rejected my God!*"

This was not to be borne. I *could not* reject Jesus.
There was only one thing to do, once I had seen the gap
behind me. *I turned away from it and flung myself over
the gap towards Jesus*.

Early on a damp English morning with spring in the
air, I wrote in the Journal and to C. S. Lewis:

I *choose* to believe in the Father, Son, and Holy Ghost – in
Christ, my Lord and my God. Christianity has the ring, the
feel, of unique truth. Of *essential* truth. By it, life is made

full instead of empty, meaningful instead of meaningless. Cosmos becomes beautiful at the *Centre*, instead of chillingly ugly beneath the lovely pathos of spring. But the emptiness, the meaninglessness, and the ugliness can only be seen, I think, when one has glimpsed the fullness, the meaning, and the beauty. It is when heaven and hell have *both* been glimpsed that going back is impossible. But to go on seemed impossible, also. A glimpse is not a vision. A choice was necessary: and there is no certainty. One can only choose a side. So I – I now choose my side: I choose beauty; I choose what I love. But choosing to believe *is* believing. It's all I can do: choose. I confess my doubts and ask my Lord Christ to enter my life. I do not *know* God is, I do but say: Be it unto me according to Thy will. I do not affirm that I am without doubt, I do but ask for help, having chosen, to overcome it. I do but say: Lord, I believe – help Thou mine unbelief.

After the great decision was made, he wrote a sonnet that summed up vividly his feelings at this time of crisis.

Did Jesus live? And did he really say
The burning words that banish mortal fear?
And are they true? Just this is central, here
The Church must stand or fall. It's Christ we weigh.

All else is off the point: the Flood, the Day
of Eden, or the Virgin Birth – Have done!
The Question is, did God send us the Son
Incarnate crying Love! Love is the Way!

Between the probable and proved there yawns
A gap. Afraid to jump, we stand absurd,
Then see behind us sink the ground and, worse,
Our very standpoint crumbling. Desperate dawns
Our only hope: to leap into the Word
That opens up the shuttered universe.

Perhaps, because I knew Sheldon as a mature student, and we keep in touch today, I may be particularly drawn to the way he states his testimony of Christ.

If "the gap" is still in front of you, but "you cannot go back" will you read John's Gospel, chapter 20 – the story of Thomas, who was slow to believe, but later steadfast in his faith, in the Deity and Resurrection glory of our Lord?

It is the classic chapter that helps us to cry "My Lord and my God", as Thomas fell at the feet of Jesus who had died, who was risen, and was at last perceived in all his radiant glory.

Your pilgrimage may be slow, but it will be steady if it leads towards Jesus. You may say along the road, "Lord, I believe, help thou my unbelief," but it will lead to saving and assured faith, if, like Thomas, you finally kneel at Christ's nail-pierced feet, look up into the Risen Christ's face, personally delineated towards you, and cry "My Lord and my God". With the great company of believers down the centuries, you will then rejoice to say humbly, boldly and assuredly, with angels and archangels and all the hosts of heaven, *"This* is our Faith." God grant it so.